Copyright © 2024 by Lucinda Mirren

All rights reserved.

No portion of this book may be reproduced in any form without written permission from the publisher or author, except as permitted by U.S. copyright law.

Contents

Section 1: – Entry level — 1

Triangle test 1
Diet suitability 3
What is the difference between specific gravity and absolute or true density 4
What is the difference between anhydrous and monohydrate 5
How to convert from mass into volume and vice versa 6
How to convert from a solution into a powder and vice versa 7
How to convert from one organic acid into another organic acid 8
How to convert from a salt (e.g., potassium sorbate) into an acid (e.g., sorbic acid) 9
How to convert from quinine base into quinine sulphate 10
How to calculate how much propylene glycol (PG) is coming from the flavours 11
Putting a recipe together 13
Caramel colourings 15
Consumer trends that impact market growth drivers 16

Section 2: – Senior level — 18

Converting single strength juice into a concentrated form 18
The role of yeast in alcohol production 23
How to name the flavours on the label 26
When is depiction allowed 27
What is the difference between flavoured versus flavour 28
Mandatory food information on the label 29

Product or legal name of the food 40
How to make an Ingredient list for label purposes 42
Allergens 43
QUID-ing (Quantitative Ingredient Declaration) on ingredients ... 45
Primary Ingredient 47
List of Additives 48
Nutrition declaration 53
Nutrition claims 58
Guidance on the use of the terms natural, pure, traditional etc. 68
Steviol Glycosides 69
Enzymes: what are they 70
How to make a final Product Specification 74

Section 3: – Management level   76

How to determine if a particular EU Regulation is still in force 76
How to construct a Product Brief 78
New Product Development Checklist 80
How to build a Procedure 82
How to put together a Process Diagram for the department 84
How to create a Training Record for the department 87
Cost saving ideas 88
How to help the environment ideas 89
NPD functionality assessment 90
Strategy for NPD department 94

Introduction – about the author

As a new product development technologist at the start of my professional career, things were not very different from now and I remember how nervous I was because of the lack of experience, a low self-confidence maybe, and the business pressure to be the best. But as a result of many years of arduous work and a continuous program of self-improvement, I have gained a great deal of skills and knowledge which I can share with you through this book. There have been challenges along the way that we all have to face through our career, but it is these challenges that propel us forward and makes us better at what we do. Today I am grateful for all the obstacles I have faced because they have given me the knowledge that I have now.

The food and drink sector has been my career for many years, and I am now a highly accomplished Manager, helping and supporting colleagues who want to start a career in this field. As an individual, I would describe myself as being highly motivated and very focused, with a strong scientific background, embraced with an Eco-Friendly approach.

DISCLAIMER:

In this book, I do not give legal advice on any matters pertaining to the food and drink industry, but instead share my own experience and knowledge that I have gained over the course of my career. It has been my goal to use the most recent legislation, and this mostly captures the EU requirements, but sometimes I have also referred to UK Guidance documents. In the interim period, between when the book was written and when it was published, there could have been changes in legislation. This book should only be used as a reference, you will need to conduct due diligence in order to ensure that you use legislation that is in force and that the product you manufacture and / or sell is legal.

The publisher and author cannot be held responsible for any errors or omissions in this book. The author and publisher disclaim all liability for any loss or damage, financial or otherwise, arising from the use of this information.

Section 1: – Entry level

Triangle test

How to perform a triangle test:

In a triangle test, two of the three samples are identical, and the taster must select the odd sample.

Each taster is assigned a different combination of letters and there are six combinations that are widely used (from 1 to 6):

CDC; CCD; CDD; DCD; DDC; DCC

TEST NUMBER: _ (from 1 to 6) __

TASTE TEST:
IDENTIFY THE ODD SAMPLE OUT

DATE: _____

NAME: _____

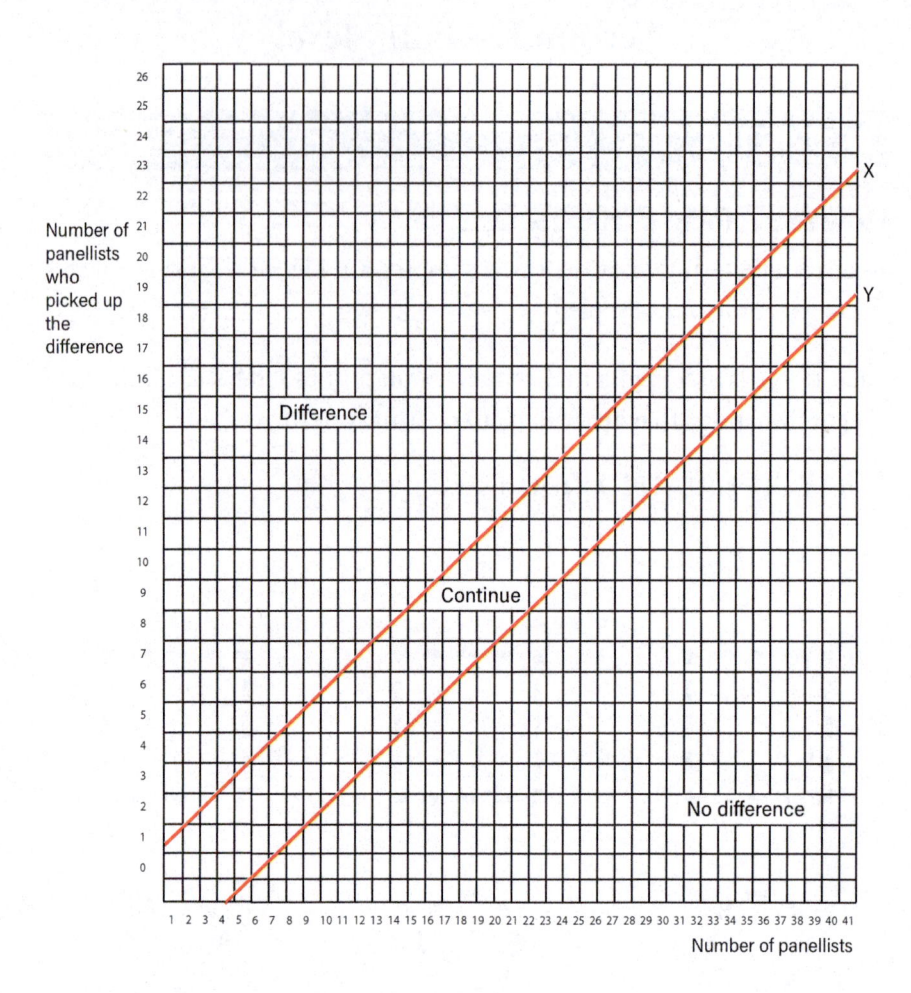

How to evaluate the triangle test results:

Above line X means that there is a difference in the organoleptic notes.

Below line Y means that there is not a difference in the organoleptic notes.

In between line X & Y means that the result is not conclusive, and you will need to expand the number of tasters.

Diet suitability

Vegan means that the product does not contain any ingredient of animal origin (mammalian, poultry, fish, crustacean, mollusc) and also it does not contain any animal derivatives (dairy, egg and bee products). This includes additives and processing aids.

Vegetarian means that the product does not contain any ingredient of animal origin (mammalian, poultry, fish, crustacean, mollusc) and also it does not contain dairy and egg products, but it can contain bee products. This includes additives and processing aids.

Ovo-Lacto Vegetarian means that the product may contain ingredients of animal origin like dairy, egg and bee products, but does not contain other ingredients of other animal origin (mammalian, poultry, fish, crustacean, mollusc). This includes additives and processing aids.

Halal suitability: It covers pork derivatives, blood derivatives that can be derived from any species of animal, ingredients that can be derived from animals, and alcohol and its derivatives.

Kosher suitability: It covers all rabbinical-approved ingredients used in the product.

What is the difference between specific gravity and absolute or true density

Although specific gravity (SG) is similar to absolute density or true density, it differs slightly. To get from specific gravity to true density, you need to multiply SG by the density of water at 20°C, which is 0.9982.

Density = Specific Gravity * 0.9982

In a scenario such as the following, you need to take into account the specific gravity values at 20°C, as well as the average value for this before you perform the conversion:

Example of specific gravity for a flavour:

Specific gravity (20/20°C): 1.0390 – 1.0490
Specific gravity (20/4°C): 1.0370 – 1.0470
Specific gravity (25/25°C): 1.0360 – 1.0460

Consequently, it will be (1.0390 + 1.0490) / 2 = 1.044

Your average SG value at 20°C is 1.044.

To determine your density, multiply this value by the density of water:

1.044 * 0.9982 = 1.042

As density is expressed in g/ml or kg/l, in our case here it is 1.042 g/ml or 1.042 kg/l.

The density or specific gravity is normally mentioned on the Ingredient Specification or Technical Data Sheet for that ingredient. Some suppliers will provide the specific gravity value, and others will provide the density value.

What is the difference between anhydrous and monohydrate

In the case of anhydrous ingredients, there is no water present, whereas in the case of monohydrate ingredients, there is one molecule of water.

Citric acid, for example, can be anhydrous (containing no water) or it can also be monohydrate (containing one molecule of water).

Citric acid anhydrous is a chemical compound with the formula $C_6H_8O_7$ and a molar mass of 192 g/mol.

Citric acid monohydrate has a molar mass of 210 g/mol, therefore, the difference of 18 is equivalent to the molar mass of one molecule of water (H_2O).

Please see below how molar mass can be calculated for a compound, in this case, citric acid anhydrous ($C_6H_8O_7$):

Firstly, you will need to know the molar mass of each atom from your compound. Either refer to the Mendeleev table or find it via the internet. Then multiply this value by the number of atoms contained in the chemical formula.

Molar mass of $C_6H_8O_7$ is: (12*6) + (1*8) + (16*7) = 192 g/mol

Where, 12 is the molar mass of carbon (C), 1 is the molar mass of hydrogen (H) and 16 is the molar mass of oxygen (O).

Another example of anhydrous versus monohydrate is glucose: glucose anhydrous and glucose monohydrate.

The molar mass of glucose anhydrous is 180 g/mol and the molar mass of glucose monohydrate is 198 g/mol. As stated previously, the difference of 18 corresponds to one molecule of water's molar mass.

How to convert from mass into volume and vice versa

The mass of an ingredient is the weight expressed as grams (g) or kilograms (kg).

Volume refers to the amount of an ingredient measured in millilitres (ml) or litres (l).

Imagine a scale when considering mass and a cylinder when considering volume, in order to better understand these concepts.

Below is an example of how mass and volume differ based on the density of the ingredient in question.

As an example, suppose you have a volume of 100 ml, and you want to convert it into mass (g). We will also assume, for argument's sake, that this ingredient has a density of 1.022 g/ml, so your equation will look as follows:

Density = Mass / Volume

Mass = Density * Volume

Mass = 1.022 * 100 = 102.2 g

If you have a mass value (102.2 g) and wish to convert this into a volume value (ml), then you will need to construct the following equation:

Density = Mass / Volume

Volume = Mass / Density

Volume = 102.2 / 1.022 = 100 ml

How to convert from a solution into a powder and vice versa

What is the difference between a solution and a powder?

This difference arises from the addition of water to make the powder a solution.

For example, if you want to convert 0.5 g of allura red solution at 1% concentration into powder, the equation will be as follows:

C% = md / ms * 100

C% = concentration percentage

md = mass of the dissolvent or mass of the powder

ms = mass of the solution

If ms is 0.5 g and C is 1 %, then md will be:

md = C * ms / 100

md = 1 * 0.5 / 100 = 0.005 g or 5 mg

Assuming you know the amount of powder (md = 0.005 g) and the concentration of the solution (C% = 1), you can calculate the mass of the solution (ms) as follows:

C% = md / ms * 100

ms = md * 100 / C%

ms = 0.005 * 100 / 1 = 0.5 g

How to convert from one organic acid into another organic acid

In this illustration I will focus on some of the organic acids, like tartaric acid, malic acid, citric acid and lactic acid.

Total acid expressed as	Tartaric Acid	Malic Acid	Citric Acid	Lactic Acid
Tartaric Acid	n/a	0.893	0.853	1.200
Malic Acid	1.119	n/a	0.955	1.344
Citric Acid	1.172	1.047	n/a	1.407
Lactic Acid	0.833	0.744	0.711	n/a

If you have 1.5 g of tartaric acid and you wish to convert it to citric acid, you multiply 1.5 by 0.853 (the value from the table under citric acid).

CA = Citric Acid

TA = Tartaric Acid

CA = TA * 0.853 = 1.5 * 0.853 = 1.28 g

As another example, if you have 2 g of malic acid, and you want to convert it into tartaric acid, then the equation will be as follows:

MA = Malic Acid

TA = Tartaric Acid

TA = MA * 1.119 = 2 * 1.119 = 2.24 g

How to convert from a salt (e.g., potassium sorbate) into an acid (e.g., sorbic acid)

It is sometimes necessary to add ingredients within your recipe in one format, then convert them into another format, as this is the means by which they are monitored and regulated by legislation. I will provide you with two examples below, one for potassium sorbate and one for sodium benzoate.

Potassium Sorbate

From a chemical standpoint, potassium sorbate is considered a salt, but from a regulatory perspective, it is regarded as a preservative. It has a chemical formula of $C_6H_7KO_2$ and a molar mass of 150 g/mol.

Sorbic acid is considered an acid, and this is the format used by legislation to monitor the actual amount of preservative being used. Sorbic acid has a chemical formula of $C_6H_8O_2$ and a molar mass of 112 g/mol.

By using their molar mass, you can convert from the salt form into the acid form. For example, if you add 0.24 g potassium sorbate to your product and you want to know how much sorbic acid this represents, then you do 0.24 * 112 / 150 = 0.18 g sorbic acid.

You can also multiply your potassium sorbate addition by 0.747, which may be a simpler method.

Sodium Benzoate

In terms of its chemical composition, sodium benzoate is a salt and a preservative for legislative purposes. It has a chemical formula of $C_7H_5NaO_2$ and a molar mass of 144 g/mol.

Benzoic acid is an acid, as the name suggests, with a chemical formula of $C_7H_6O_2$ and a molar mass of 122 g/mol.

To convert from salt to acid, multiply your sodium benzoate addition by 122 and divide by 144.

Or another way is to multiply your sodium benzoate addition by 0.85.

How to convert from quinine base into quinine sulphate

The bitter taste of tonic drinks is caused by quinine, a component that may be found in tonic flavours. It was first extracted from the cinchona tree and used to treat malaria.

In the case of developing tonic water, for example, if you wish to convert quinine base into quinine sulphate, you may use their molar mass to do so, and I will provide an example below.

Let's suppose your tonic water uses 1 g of the tonic flavour that contains 6% quinine base.

We know that:

Quinine base has a chemical formula of $C_{20}H_{24}N_2O_2$ and a molar mass of 324 g/mol.

Quinine sulphate has a chemical formula of $C_{20}H_{26}N_2O_6S$ and a molar mass of 422 g/mol.

6% means that you have 6 g quinine base in 100 g tonic flavour.

Therefore, the calculation is as follows:

6 * 1 / 100 = 0.06 g quinine base in 1 g tonic flavour

0.06 * 422 / 324 = 0.078 g or 78 mg quinine sulphate in 1 g tonic flavour

How to calculate how much propylene glycol (PG) is coming from the flavours

In the food & drink sector, propylene glycol can be used as a solvent within the manufacturing process of flavourings. According to EU regulation, there is a maximum limit that must be adhered to.

Propylene glycol levels permitted in food and beverages in the EU may differ from those in other parts of the world and in some areas of the globe it is not regulated at all.

The following example illustrates how to calculate the amount of propylene glycol (PG) in a product.

Suppose you are making a soft drink and you use two flavours that contain propylene glycol, but none of the other ingredients contain propylene glycol. For argument's sake, let's say one flavour is strawberry and the other one is raspberry.

Let's say the strawberry contains 30% PG (information that you can normally find on the Ingredient Specification), while the raspberry contains 45% PG.

The strawberry is used in 1 g/l soft drink and the raspberry is used in 0.5 g/l soft drink.

Therefore, you will have:

30 * 1 / 100 = 0.3 g PG/l soft drink–coming from the strawberry flavour

and

45 * 0.5 / 100 = 0.225 g PG/l soft drink–coming from the raspberry flavour

Total will be 0.3 + 0.225 = 0.525 g PG/l soft drink.

The legal limit for PG in soft drinks in the EU is 1 g/l (from all sources, not just flavourings), so the value above is within the legal limit.

Here is a link to the Regulation (EC) 1333/2008 relating to the propylene glycol limit. I have provided a screenshot as well.

http://tiny.cc/susrxz

PART 4 – Food additives including carriers in food flavourings

Beeswax	Flavourings in non-alcoholic flavoured drinks	200 mg/l in flavoured drinks
Triethyl citrate	All flavourings	3 000 mg/kg from all sources in foodstuffs as consumed or as reconstituted according to the instructions of the manufacturer; individually or in combination. In the case of beverages, with the exception of cream liqueurs, the maximum level of E 1520 shall be 1 000 mg/l from all sources
Glyceryl diacetate (diacetin)		
Glyceryl triacetate (triacetin)		
Propane-1, 2-diol (propylene glycol)		
Benzyl alcohol	Flavourings for:	
	— liqueurs, aromatised wines, aromatised wine-based drinks and aromatised	100 mg/l in final food

Putting a recipe together

We all approach recipes differently, depending on the industry in which we work and how we were trained.

Below is a simple example of how I put a recipe together for a non-alcoholic drink. A column is dedicated to ingredients, one to volume, one to mass and another one to density. I use true density as opposed to specific gravity, as I have previously mentioned in my book. If the Ingredient Specification makes reference to specific gravity rather than true density, then I do the conversion accordingly.

Ingredients	Volume (Litres)	Mass (Kilograms)	Density
Liquid Sugar	150	199	1.3295
Orange Juice Concentrate	6.9	9.0	1.3040
Citric Acid	4.2	6.5	1.5400
Vitamin Premix	3.6	5.5	1.5400
Ginseng Extract	1.1	1.1	0.9760
Caramel Colouring	0.2	0.3	1.3300
Flavour	0.9	1.0	1.0980
Demineralised Water	833	832	0.9982
Total	**1000**	**1054**	

Depending on the ingredient type, some may be added in kilograms (as mass) and others in litres (as volume). When doing a recipe, you need to ensure that the ingredients are added in the correct dosage and when they are combined, they yield the batch size you anticipated.

There are some ingredients which can be added straight into the main tank or mixing bowl, while others should ideally be dissolved in water first, prior to addition to the mixing bowl. Generally speaking, high dosage ingredients are added directly to the main tank, while smaller dose ingredients (acids, preservatives, flavours, colours etc.) are dissolved first in water in a smaller tank or container before being added to the main tank. This can depend on the industry you work in and the manufacturing practices that you follow.

When ingredients are added in high dosages, the recipe will not require decimal places since the difference between adding, for example 150 litres of liquid sugar to 1000 litres of drink and adding 149.68 litres of liquid sugar to 1000 litres is negligible. Obviously, for ingredients that are added in small dosage the decimals are needed for better accuracy and you may need to use one, two, or even three decimals, depending on the ingredient itself and the batch size.

Caramel colourings

Caramel colourings, as the name implies, are used to colour food and beverage products. They are normally made from glucose syrup and can have a colloidal charge. For the development of a product, it is imperative to consider the colloidal charge of your ingredients, as for example, if you use a caramel colour with an inappropriate colloidal charge in a drink, sediment will form, and the liquid will appear hazy.

I have included the four different types or classes below, along with how they can be labelled within the Ingredient list.

Colour E 150a (EU)

Other names:
Colour Plain Caramel (EU)
Colour [150a] (Australia / New Zealand)
Caramel Color (USA)

Colour E 150b (EU)

Other names:
Colour Caustic Sulphite Caramel (EU)
Colour [150b] (Australia / New Zealand)
Caramel Color (USA)

Colour E 150c (EU)

Other names:
Colour Ammonia Caramel (EU)
Colour [150c] (Australia / New Zealand)
Caramel Color (USA)

Colour E 150d (EU)

Other names:
Colour Sulphite Ammonia Caramel (EU)
Colour [150d] (Australia / New Zealand)
Caramel Color (USA)

Consumer trends that impact market growth drivers

Contributions to social welfare

Consumption trends are shifting towards ethical consumerism, with end users increasingly placing an emphasis on socially responsible businesses that respect people throughout the supply chain.

Experiencing food

Food has become an adventure for shoppers today, whether it is through the introduction of new flavours, textures and colours, or through joining in on the creation process, which can provide deeper levels of engagement.

Premiumisation

The public is looking for core products with a premium twist that have a superior taste profile and provenance.

Exotic

The consumer is hungry for new food and drink experiences that are exotic and linked to health credentials.

Eco-Friendly Production

Modern individuals expect innovative, technology-driven solutions that go beyond simply reducing waste and resources to ones that repair and rebuild the environment.

An engaging and memorable approach

There is a growing trend among buyers to seek out tasty and adventurous food and drinks that evoke feelings of comfort and nostalgia.

Integrity and traceability

As customers look for authentic and trustworthy manufacturers, the demand for verifiable assurances regarding what ingredients go in the products, where they come from, and who made them, is increasing.

Maintaining a balanced lifestyle

A synergistic approach to health and wellbeing has gained prominence throughout the market, where physical and mental health are intertwined and eating well is beneficial to both.

After experiencing lockdowns, consumers wish to escape the confines of their home and explore, play, and experience new things. The end users are seeking food and beverages with clean, clear labels and ingredients that emphasize flavours, colours, and textures. They are considering innovative and exciting ways of tapping into more occasions throughout the day or between meals, based on their individual lifestyle.

Section 2: – Senior level

Converting single strength juice into a concentrated form

Using the example below, I calculated the amount of apple juice as concentrate (in volume) that I would need in 1000 ml of beverage to achieve 100% (in volume) juice as single strength.

The following values are needed in order to perform the calculation:
- Corrected Brix value of the concentrate
- Corrected Brix value of the single strength juice
- Specific gravity of the concentrate
- Specific gravity of the single strength juice
- Density of water at 20 degrees Celsius

Corrected Brix value of the concentrate – can usually be found on the Ingredient Specification. Some suppliers give two values for Brix – one for uncorrected Brix and one for corrected Brix. I use the value for corrected Brix for the reasons listed below.

A significant amount of soluble organic acids, such as citric acid, are present in fruit juices, affecting the refractometer reading in terms of the total dissolved solids content. This means that the high soluble acid component of fruit juices refracts light differently to sucrose solutions for which the equipment was calibrated. This will result in an error in the Brix reading and as a result, the reading in reality will be lower. Therefore, an acidity correction must be added to the Brix reading when measuring fruit juices with a high acidity level.

Corrected Brix value of the single strength juice – this can be found in Annex V of Directive 2012/12/EU, amending Council Directive 2001/112/EC relating to fruit juices and certain similar products intended for human consumption, please see screenshots of this on the following pages.

Specific gravity of the concentrate – this can be on the Ingredient Specification or in the Domke tables.

Specific gravity of the single strength juice – this can be on the Ingredient Specification as well or in the Domke tables. In my calculation I use Domke tables to determine specific gravity based on the corrected Brix value of the single strength juice. I then convert specific gravity into true density.

(For copyright reasons, I have not included the Domke tables in this book).

The **density of water at 20 degrees Celsius** is 0.9982. (You might find other documents or papers which use a slightly different name and value for this).

Corrected Brix values of the single strength juice or minimum Brix levels for reconstituted fruit juice (Annex V).
http://tiny.cc/qwsrxz

ANNEX V

MINIMUM BRIX LEVELS FOR RECONSTITUTED FRUIT JUICE AND RECONSTITUTED FRUIT PURÉE

Common Name of the Fruit	Botanical Name	Minimum Brix levels
Apple (*)	*Malus domestica* Borkh.	11,2
Apricot (**)	*Prunus armeniaca* L.	11,2
Banana (**)	*Musa x paradisiaca* L. (excluding plantains)	21,0
Blackcurrant (*)	*Ribes nigrum* L.	11,0
Grape (*)	*Vitis vinifera* L. or hybrids thereof	15,9

Grape (*)	*Vitis vinifera* L. or hybrids thereof *Vitis labrusca* L. or hybrids thereof	15,9
Grapefruit (*)	*Citrus x paradisi* Macfad.	10,0
Guava (**)	*Psidium guajava* L.	8,5
Lemon (*)	*Citrus limon* (L.) Burm.f.	8,0
Mango (**)	*Mangifera indica* L.	13,5
Orange (*)	*Citrus sinensis* (L.) Osbeck	11,2
Passion Fruit (*)	*Passiflora edulis* Sims	12,0
Peach (**)	*Prunus persica* (L.) Batsch var. persica	10,0
Pear (**)	*Pyrus communis* L.	11,9
Pineapple (*)	*Ananas comosus* (L.) Merr.	12,8
Raspberry (*)	*Rubus idaeus* L.	7,0
Sour Cherry (*)	*Prunus cerasus* L.	13,5
Strawberry (*)	*Fragaria x ananassa* Duch.	7,0
Tomato (*)	*Lycopersicon esculentum*, Mill.	5,0
Mandarin (*)	*Citrus reticulata* Blanco	11,2

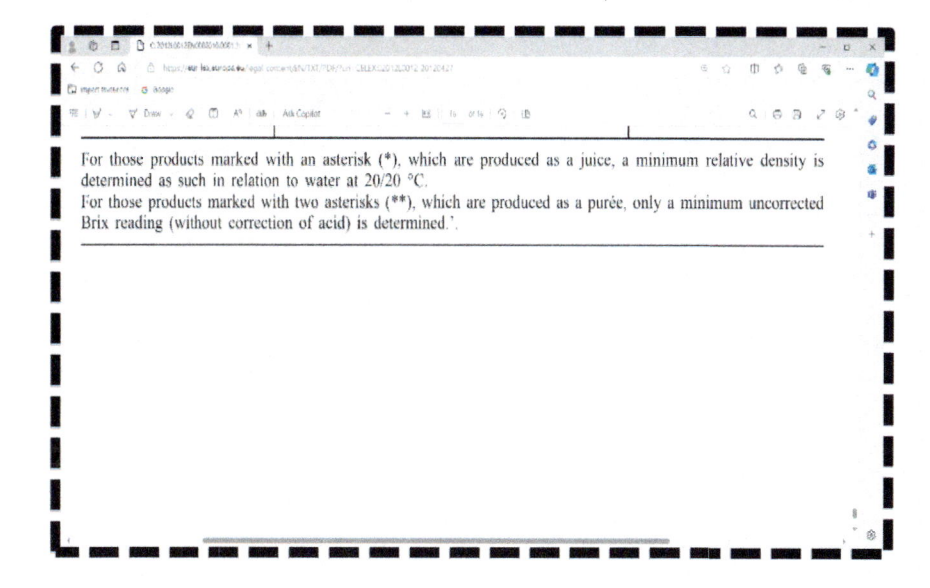

For those products marked with an asterisk (*), which are produced as a juice, a minimum relative density is determined as such in relation to water at 20/20 °C.
For those products marked with two asterisks (**), which are produced as a purée, only a minimum uncorrected Brix reading (without correction of acid) is determined.'.

Using our example, the % juice as single strength required is 100 (per 1000 ml beverage).

Corrected Brix value of the apple juice as concentrate	70.65
Corrected Brix value of the apple juice as single strength	11.2
Specific gravity of the apple juice as concentrate	1.3539
Specific gravity of the apple juice as single strength	1.045
Density of water at 20 degrees Celsius	0.9982

The calculation is as follows:

100% volume juice as single strength = 1000 ml juice as single strength in 1000 ml rtd

1000 * (1.045 * 0.9982) = 1043 g juice as single strength per 1000 ml rtd

1043 / (70.65 / 11.2) = 165.36 g juice as concentrate per 1000 ml rtd

165.36 / (1.3539 * 0.9982) = 122.36 ml juice as concentrate per 1000 ml rtd

This is one method of calculation, I will show you another below. You can use either method or both to see if they produce similar results. This method is based on grams of solids per litre rtd and it is as follows:

(VSSJ * BxSSJ * SGSSJ * DW) / 100 = grams of solids per litre

Where,

VSSJ is volume of single strength juice

BxSSJ is Brix of single strength juice

SGSSJ is specific gravity of single strength juice

DW is density of water at 20 degrees Celsius

Therefore,

(1000 * 11.2 * 1.045 * 0.9982) / 100 = 116.83 g of solids per litre

116.83 * 100 / 70.65 = 165.36 g juice as concentrate per 1000 ml rtd

165.36 / (1.3539 * 0.9982) = 122.36 ml juice as concentrate per 1000 ml rtd

The role of yeast in alcohol production

Yeasts are single-celled organisms that belong to the fungus kingdom. While some of these yeasts have beneficial properties, others are classed as pathogenic, therefore not desirable. The food and drink sectors make extensive use of beneficial yeasts, the most common of which are bakery and alcohol production. Our focus in this book will be on the production of alcohol alone.

Yeast is used in a wide range of alcohol manufacturing applications, including wine, cider, beer and more. Similarly, spirits, which are distilled ferments, are initially made by fermenting yeast.

During the fermentation process yeast feeds on fermentable sugars and converts them into alcohol. Some yeasts can produce alcohol up to 14% alcohol by volume, and some can produce as high as 20%. Additionally, depending on the yeast used, the ferment may differ from an organoleptic standpoint, since this significantly affects the fermentation's chemical composition. Among the by-products of the process are heat and carbon dioxide.

Since yeast is a living organism, optimal working conditions are imperative to achieving good results, and nutrient levels, pH, and temperature are some of the most important parameters to consider. As a result, if these parameters are not optimal, fermentation may be difficult or undesirable off notes may arise, which might result in an adverse effect on the organoleptic profile, or worse, you may end up with an unusable ferment.

In the following example I have included a yeast strain used to produce cider, together with instructions for use and a draft recipe:

In a nutshell, **cider** is a product which:
- is obtained by fermenting apple or pear juice;
- meets the requirements for juice content;
- contains less than 8.5% alcohol by volume;
- has been produced without the addition of another alcoholic product, or any substance other than a permitted one, which imparts colour or flavour.

http://tiny.cc/uwsrxz

Ingredients:
Active dry yeast Saccharomyces cerevisiae, E491

Instruction for use:
- recommended yeast dosage: 25-50 g/hL;
- rehydrate yeast in 10 times its weight in clean chlorine free water at a temperature between 35° and 40°C;
- stir gently to dissolve and allow to stand for 20 minutes;
- mix the rehydrated yeast with a little juice mixture, gradually adjusting the yeast suspension temperature to within 5-10°C of the juice blend temperature;
- inoculate the adjusted yeast suspension into the juice mixture;
- have the cooling tank jacket set point temperature at 26°C.

Ingredients	1000L batch
Pear juice concentrate	100 kg
Glucose syrup	242 kg
Diammonium phosphate	0.5 kg
Yeast nutrient mix	0.035 kg
Glucoamylase	0.022 kg
Potassium metabisulphite	0.1 kg
Yeast	0.3 kg
Chlorine free water	to 1000 L

Using this example recipe as a basis for calculation, I will demonstrate below what the expected alcohol content by volume should be:

As a rule, 17 g fermentable sugars yield 1% alcohol by volume (abv%).

In this example, the pear juice concentrate has 68 g carbohydrate / 100 g juice. Glucose syrup has 71 g carbohydrate / 100 g syrup.

Therefore, the calculation is as follows:

100 * 68 / 100 = 68 g carbohydrate in our recipe, coming from the pear juice concentrate

242 * 71 / 100 = 172 g carbohydrate in our recipe, coming from the glucose syrup

A carbohydrate may contain small amounts of higher chain sugars that yeast is unable to access, but this will be converted by glucoamylase into smaller chain sugars.

68 / 17 = 4% alcohol coming from the pear juice conversion

172 / 17 = 10% alcohol coming from the glucose syrup conversion

Therefore, total alcohol yield in the pear ferment is 14% (4% + 10%).

Within the ferment, each ingredient has a specific function to perform, and this is captured in more detail here:

- pear juice and glucose syrup contain fermentable sugars that get converted into alcohol with the aid of yeast;
- diammonium phosphate and yeast nutrient mix provide valuable food for yeast to develop and thrive;
- glucoamylase is an enzyme capable of cutting starch, liberating single glucose units that yeast can use;
- potassium metabisulphite is a preservative, and it is added so the wild yeast growth is minimised and controlled;
- untreated water provides yeast with a greater supply of nutrients to feed on, resulting in a better performance.

How to name the flavours on the label

Flavours in the food and beverage sector can be classified into the following categories (for the United Kingdom market):

Natural X Flavouring – at least 95% weight / weight of the flavouring component comes from the named source material. These flavours are normally referred to as FTNS (from the named source) or FTNF (from the named fruit).

Natural X Flavouring with other natural flavourings – at least 51% weight / weight of the flavouring component comes from the depicted source. The usual abbreviation for these flavours is WONF (with other natural flavourings).

Natural Flavouring – there is less than 51% weight / weight of the flavouring component coming from the mentioned source matter.

Flavourings which cannot be described as natural – as the name suggests, these flavours can't be described as natural because they don't meet this criteria.

Flavourings – for ease, all of the above four categories can use the term flavourings, regardless of their status.

The following example illustrates a raspberry flavour for each of the above flavour categories and how you should call this within the Ingredient list:

Natural X Flavouring:
Natural raspberry flavouring *or* Flavouring

Natural X Flavouring with other natural flavourings:
Natural raspberry flavouring with other natural flavourings *or* Flavouring

Natural Flavouring (raspberry):
Natural flavouring *or* Flavouring

Flavourings which cannot be described as natural (raspberry):
Flavouring

When is depiction allowed

Decision diagram on flavour depiction:

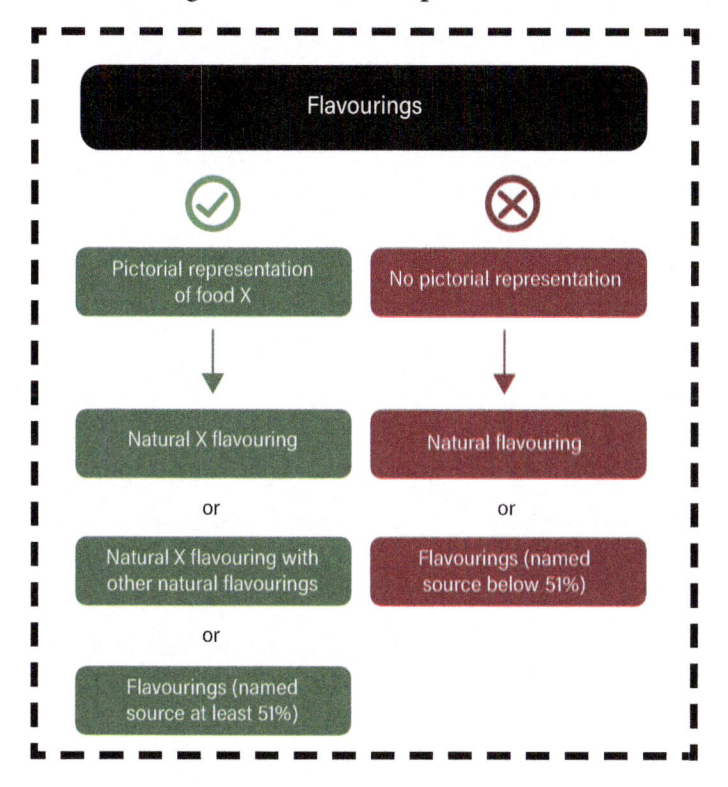

```
                        Flavourings
                    ✓              ✗
        Pictorial representation    No pictorial representation
              of food X
                    ↓                       ↓
          Natural X flavouring        Natural flavouring
                   or                        or
        Natural X flavouring with    Flavourings (named
        other natural flavourings    source below 51%)
                   or
         Flavourings (named
         source at least 51%)
```

UK flavour guidance is available at the following link:

https://www.fdf.org.uk/globalassets/resources/publications/pictorial-representation-guidance.pdf

This explains in detail when flavour depiction is allowed, as well as when it is permitted based on the presence of both, food ingredients and flavourings.

Moreover, Article 7 of Regulation (EU) No 1169/2011 on the provision of food information to consumers provides advice on how to avoid misleading consumers and I have provided a link for this below.

http://tiny.cc/gvsrxz

What is the difference between flavoured versus flavour

The term *X flavoured* can be used in the name of a food or beverage where that food or beverage contains the food ingredient of flavour X or where the food or beverage contains a flavouring obtained from the food ingredient flavour of X:

Where *natural X flavouring* is used or
Where *natural X flavouring with other natural flavourings* is used or
Where *flavouring* which is derived wholly or mainly from X flavour is used

Examples:
Natural raspberry flavouring
Natural raspberry with other natural flavourings
Flavouring (a raspberry flavour that it is not classed as natural, but it has at least 51% real raspberry in)

This category allows for depictions on the label.

The term *X flavour* can be used when a food or beverage has the flavour of X, but does not contain X.

Where *natural flavouring* is used or
Where *flavouring* which is not derived wholly or mainly from X flavour is used

Examples:
Natural flavouring (a raspberry flavour that it is classed as natural, and it has less than 51% real raspberry in)
Flavouring (a raspberry flavour that it is not classed as natural, and it has less than 51% real raspberry in)

This category does not allow for depictions on the label.

Mandatory food information on the label

It is mandatory that you include the following information on the label:
- The name of your food;
- A list with your ingredients;
- Any ingredient or processing aid that is classed as an allergen or if it could cause intolerances and may still be present in the finished product;
- The percentage of particular ingredients or categories of ingredients (QUID);
- The net quantity of your food;
- The date of minimum durability or the 'use by' date;
- Any special conditions for storage and/or use;
- The business name and address of the food business operator;
- The country of origin or place of provenance. Please refer to Article 26 of Regulation (EU) No 1169/2011 for more information;
- Guidance of how the food/drink should be used if an absence of such guidance would make it difficult to make appropriate use of it;
- For drinks with more than 1.2% alcohol by volume there is a need to mention the alcoholic strength by volume;
- A nutrition declaration. Exempted foods from the mandatory nutrition declaration are captured in Annex V of Regulation (EU) No 1169/2011.

The labelling of certain foods must include additional information, see this below:
- Foods packaged in certain gases
- Foods containing sweeteners
- Foods containing glycyrrhizinic acid or its ammonium salt
- Beverages with high caffeine content or foods with added caffeine
- Foods with added phytosterols, phytosterol esters, phytostanols or phytostanol esters
- Frozen meat, frozen meat preparations and frozen unprocessed

fishery products

In Annex III of Regulation (EU) No 1169/2011, link and also screenshots below, the above-mentioned food categories are specifically addressed:

http://tiny.cc/ivsrxz

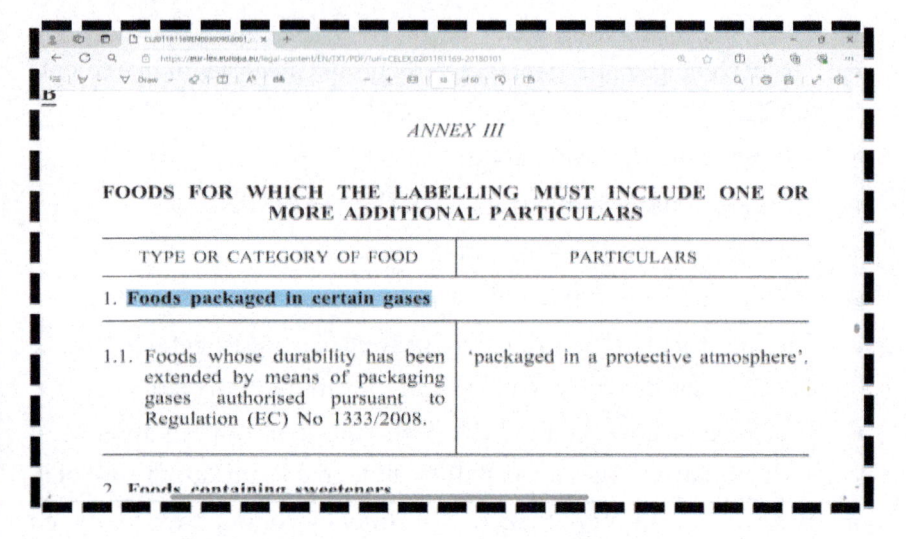

Foods packaged in certain gases

ANNEX III

FOODS FOR WHICH THE LABELLING MUST INCLUDE ONE OR MORE ADDITIONAL PARTICULARS

TYPE OR CATEGORY OF FOOD	PARTICULARS
1. **Foods packaged in certain gases**	
1.1. Foods whose durability has been extended by means of packaging gases authorised pursuant to Regulation (EC) No 1333/2008.	'packaged in a protective atmosphere'.
2. Foods containing sweeteners	

Foods containing sweeteners

2. **Foods containing sweeteners**	
2.1. Foods containing a sweetener or sweeteners authorised pursuant to Regulation (EC) No 1333/2008.	'with sweetener(s)' this statement shall accompany the name of the food.
2.2. Foods containing both an added sugar or sugars and a sweetener or sweeteners authorised pursuant to Regulation (EC) No 1333/2008.	'with sugar(s) and sweetener(s)' this statement shall accompany the name of the food.

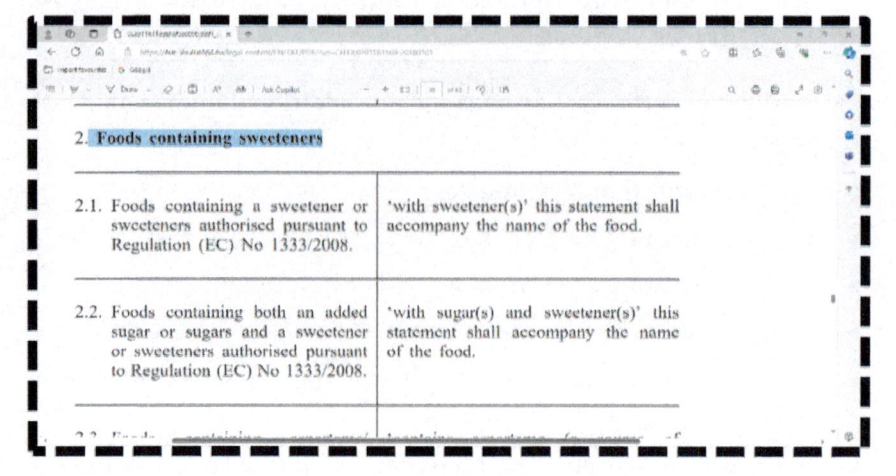

2.3.	Foods containing aspartame/ aspartame-acesulfame salt authorised pursuant to Regulation EC) No 1333/2008.	'contains aspartame (a source of phenylalanine)' shall appear on the label in cases where aspartame/ aspartame-acesulfame salt is designated in the list of ingredients only by reference to the E number. 'contains a source of phenylalanine' shall appear on the label in cases where aspartame/aspartame-acesulfame salt is designated in the list of ingredients by its specific name.
2.4.	Foods containing more than 10 % added polyols authorised pursuant to Regulation (EC) No 1333/2008.	'excessive consumption may produce laxative effects'.

Foods containing glycyrrhizinic acid or its ammonium salt

3. Foods containing glycyrrhizinic acid or its ammonium salt

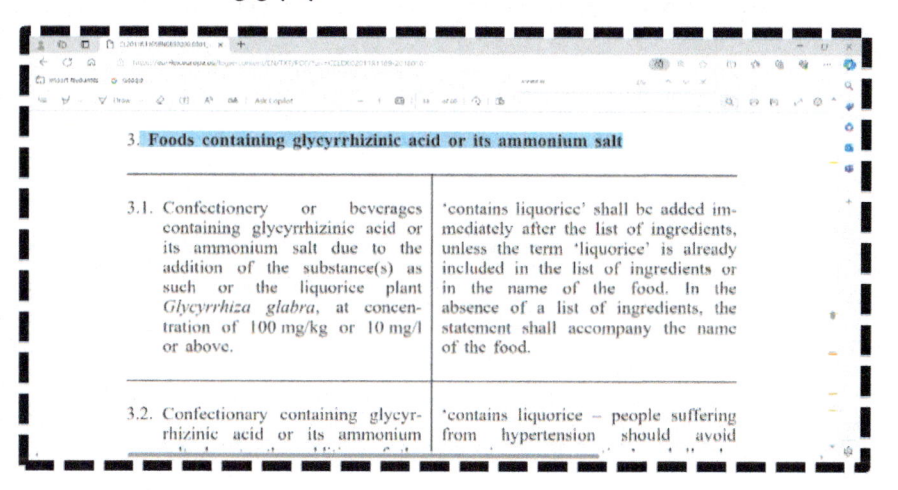

3.1.	Confectionery or beverages containing glycyrrhizinic acid or its ammonium salt due to the addition of the substance(s) as such or the liquorice plant *Glycyrrhiza glabra*, at concentration of 100 mg/kg or 10 mg/l or above.	'contains liquorice' shall be added immediately after the list of ingredients, unless the term 'liquorice' is already included in the list of ingredients or in the name of the food. In the absence of a list of ingredients, the statement shall accompany the name of the food.
3.2.	Confectionary containing glycyrrhizinic acid or its ammonium	'contains liquorice – people suffering from hypertension should avoid

or above.	of the food.
3.2. Confectionary containing glycyrrhizinic acid or its ammonium salt due to the addition of the substance(s) as such or the liquorice plant *Glycyrrhiza glabra* at concentrations of 4 g/kg or above.	'contains liquorice – people suffering from hypertension should avoid excessive consumption' shall be added immediately after the list of ingredients. In the absence of a list of ingredients, the statement shall accompany the name of the food.

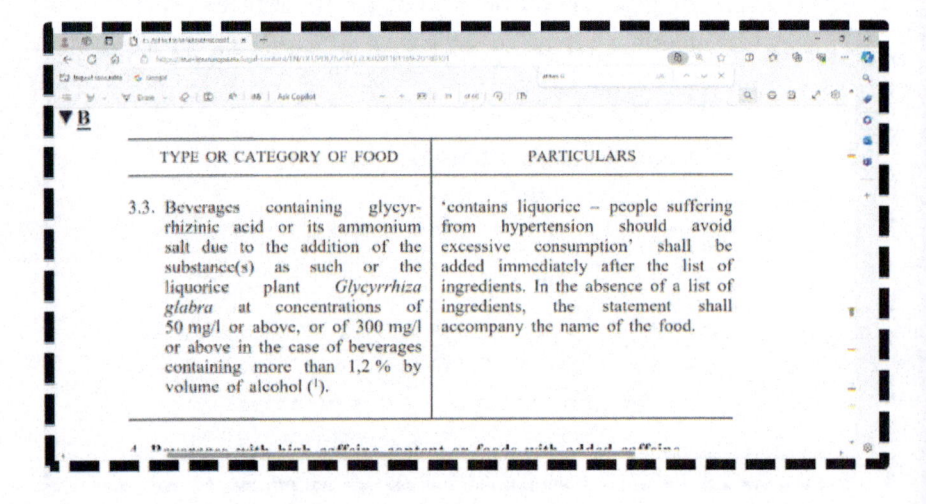

B

TYPE OR CATEGORY OF FOOD	PARTICULARS
3.3. Beverages containing glycyrrhizinic acid or its ammonium salt due to the addition of the substance(s) as such or the liquorice plant *Glycyrrhiza glabra* at concentrations of 50 mg/l or above, or of 300 mg/l or above in the case of beverages containing more than 1,2 % by volume of alcohol ([1]).	'contains liquorice – people suffering from hypertension should avoid excessive consumption' shall be added immediately after the list of ingredients. In the absence of a list of ingredients, the statement shall accompany the name of the food.

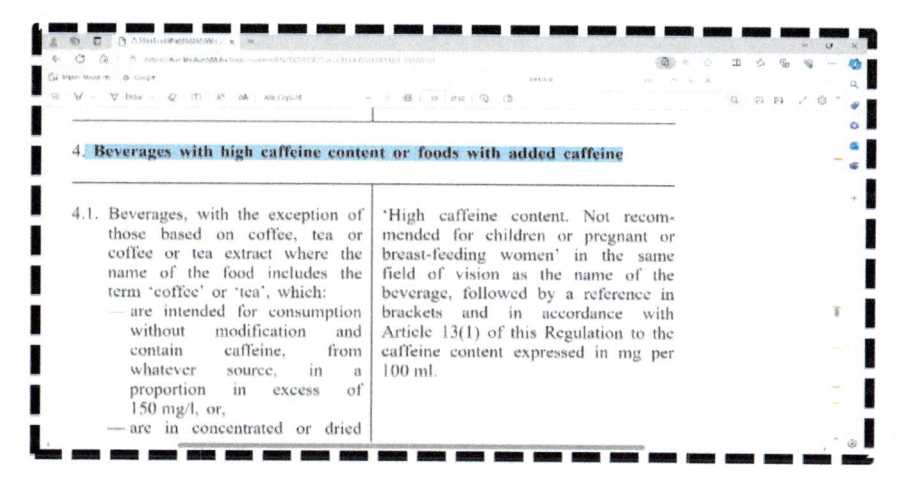

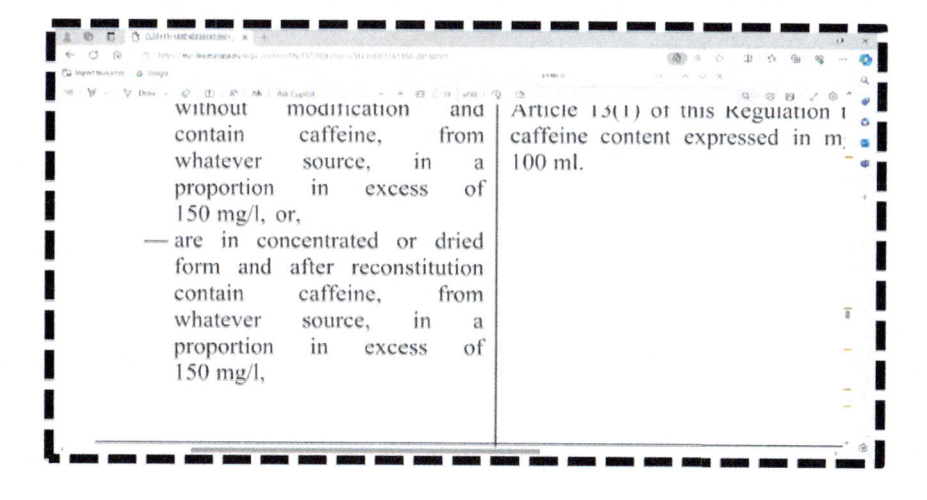

Beverages with high caffeine content or foods with added caffeine

4. Beverages with high caffeine content or foods with added caffeine

4.1. Beverages, with the exception of those based on coffee, tea or coffee or tea extract where the name of the food includes the term 'coffee' or 'tea', which: — are intended for consumption without modification and contain caffeine, from whatever source, in a proportion in excess of 150 mg/l, or, — are in concentrated or dried form and after reconstitution contain caffeine, from whatever source, in a proportion in excess of 150 mg/l,	'High caffeine content. Not recommended for children or pregnant or breast-feeding women' in the same field of vision as the name of the beverage, followed by a reference in brackets and in accordance with Article 13(1) of this Regulation to the caffeine content expressed in mg per 100 ml.

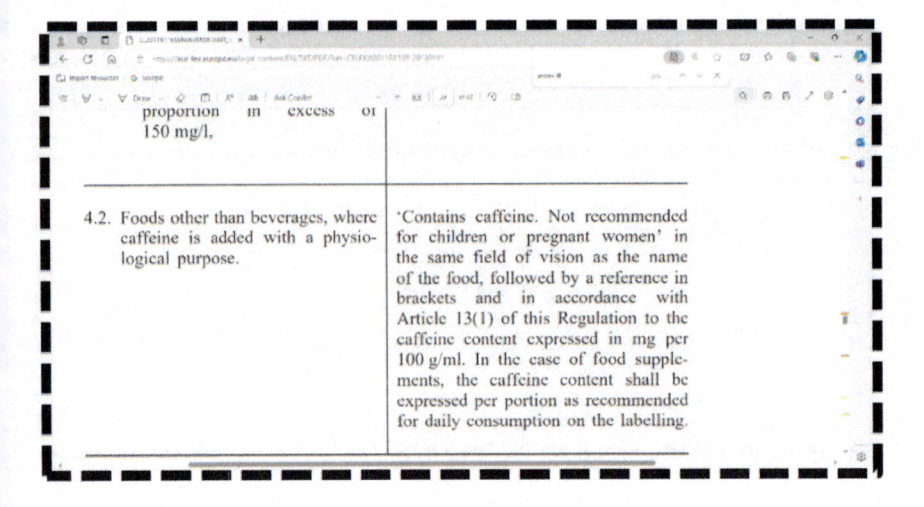

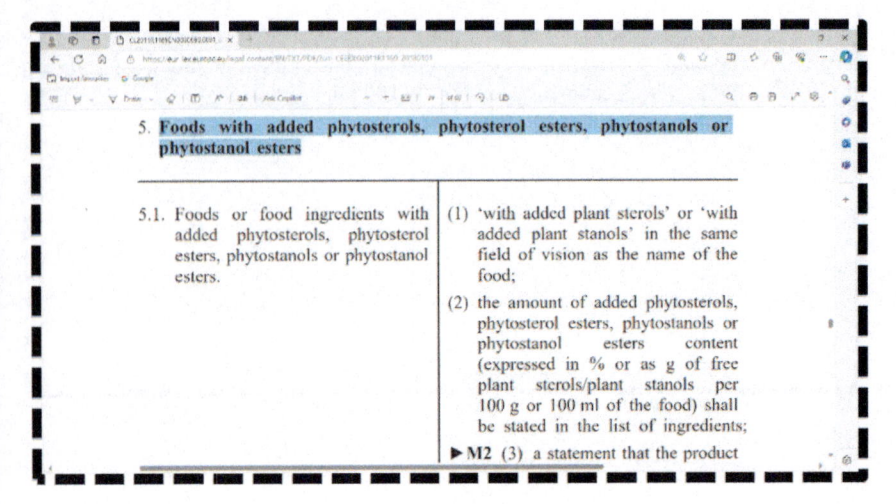

proportion in excess of 150 mg/l.	
4.2. Foods other than beverages, where caffeine is added with a physiological purpose.	'Contains caffeine. Not recommended for children or pregnant women' in the same field of vision as the name of the food, followed by a reference in brackets and in accordance with Article 13(1) of this Regulation to the caffeine content expressed in mg per 100 g/ml. In the case of food supplements, the caffeine content shall be expressed per portion as recommended for daily consumption on the labelling.

Foods with added phytosterols, phytosterol esters, phytostanols or phytostanol esters

5.	**Foods with added phytosterols, phytosterol esters, phytostanols or phytostanol esters**	
5.1.	Foods or food ingredients with added phytosterols, phytosterol esters, phytostanols or phytostanol esters.	(1) 'with added plant sterols' or 'with added plant stanols' in the same field of vision as the name of the food;
		(2) the amount of added phytosterols, phytosterol esters, phytostanols or phytostanol esters content (expressed in % or as g of free plant sterols/plant stanols per 100 g or 100 ml of the food) shall be stated in the list of ingredients;
		▶M2 (3) a statement that the product

be stated in the list of ingredients;

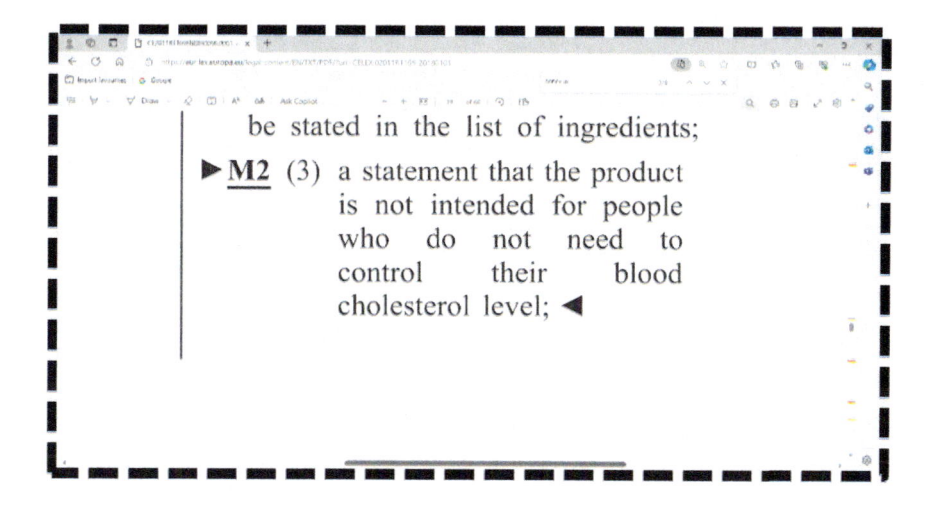

▶ __M2__ (3) a statement that the product is not intended for people who do not need to control their blood cholesterol level; ◀

TYPE OR CATEGORY OF FOOD	PARTICULARS
	(4) a statement that patients on cholesterol lowering medication should only consume the product under medical supervision;
	(5) an easily visible statement that the food may not be nutritionally appropriate for pregnant or breast-feeding women and children under the age of 5 years;
	(6) advice that the food is to be used

35

(6) advice that the food is to be used as part of a balanced and varied diet, including regular consumption of fruit and vegetables to help maintain carotenoid levels;

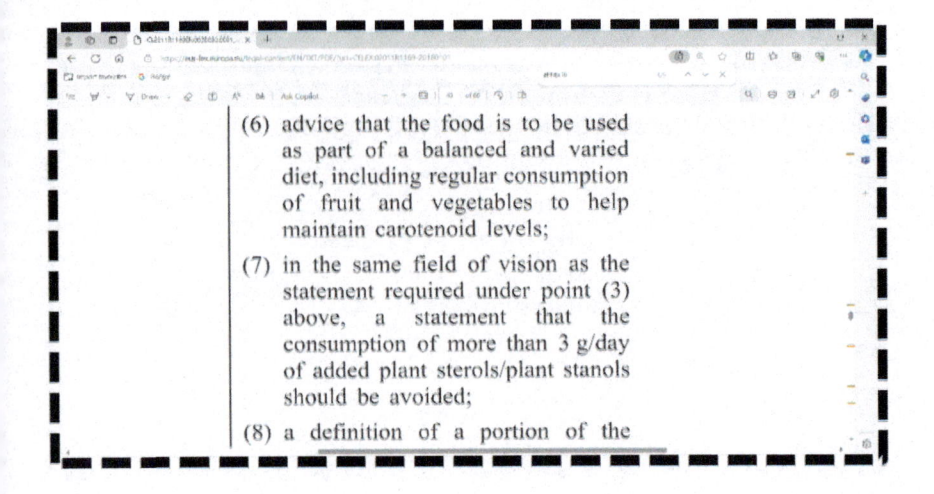

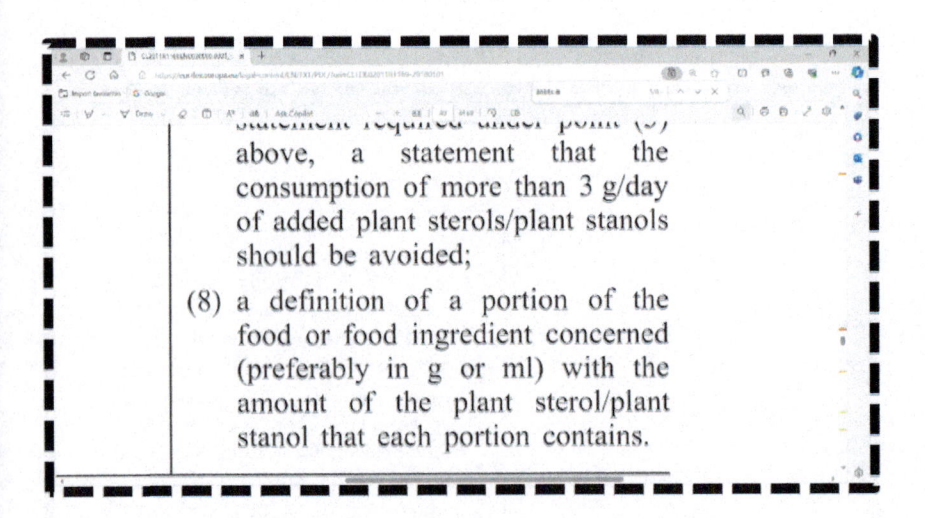

(7) in the same field of vision as the statement required under point (3) above, a statement that the consumption of more than 3 g/day of added plant sterols/plant stanols should be avoided;

(8) a definition of a portion of the food or food ingredient concerned (preferably in g or ml) with the amount of the plant sterol/plant stanol that each portion contains.

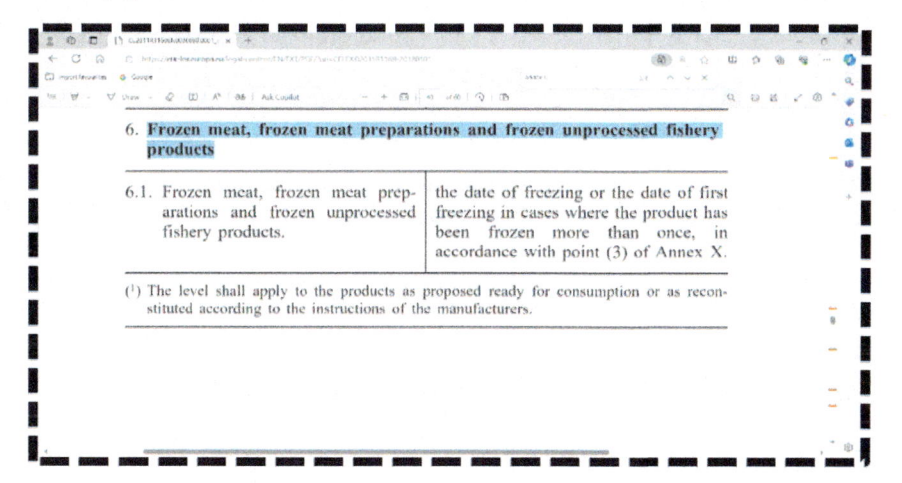

Frozen meat, frozen meat preparations and frozen unprocessed fishery products

6. **Frozen meat, frozen meat preparations and frozen unprocessed fishery products**

6.1. Frozen meat, frozen meat preparations and frozen unprocessed fishery products.	the date of freezing or the date of first freezing in cases where the product has been frozen more than once, in accordance with point (3) of Annex X.

([1]) The level shall apply to the products as proposed ready for consumption or as reconstituted according to the instructions of the manufacturers.

Colours

There is mandatory information on some colours as well and this is captured under Regulation (EC) 1333/2008 on food additives, Annex V, link and screenshot provided below.

http://tiny.cc/kvsrxz

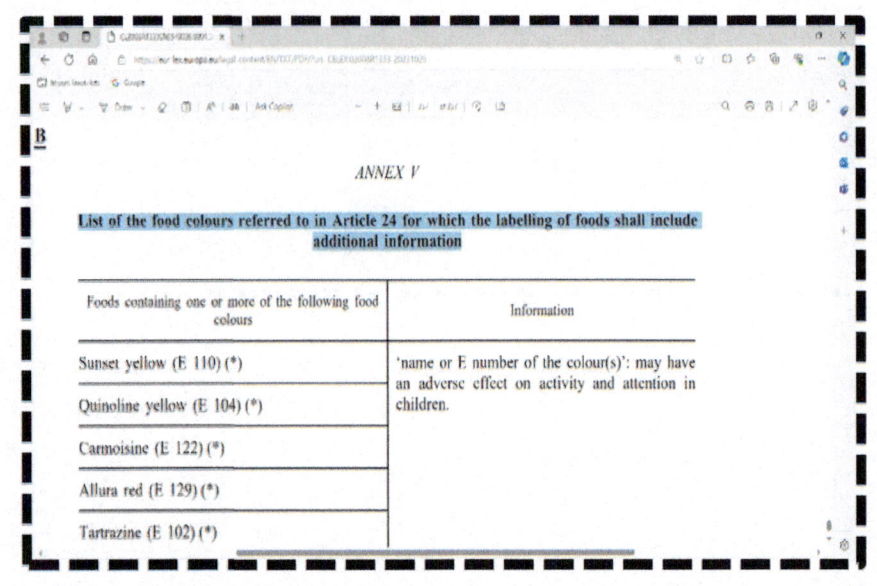

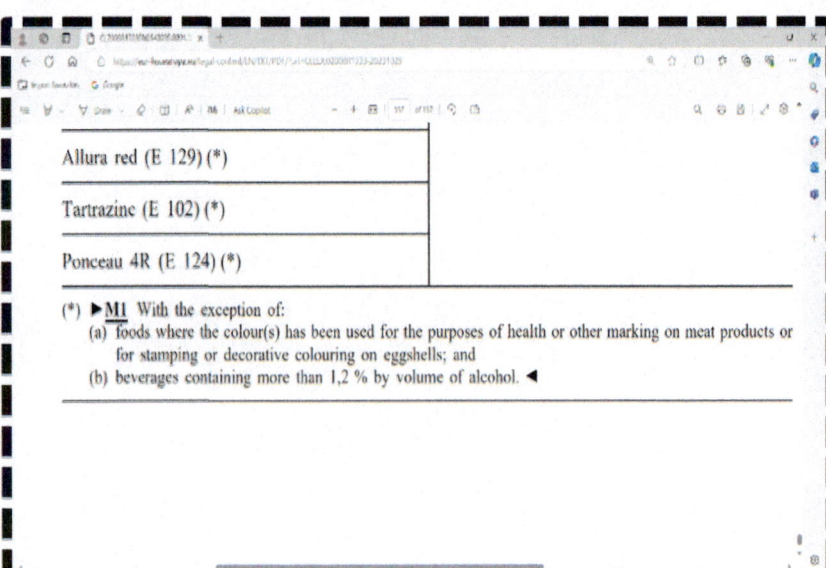

ANNEX V

List of the food colours referred to in Article 24 for which the labelling of foods shall include additional information

Foods containing one or more of the following food colours	Information
Sunset yellow (E 110) (*)	'name or E number of the colour(s)': may have an adverse effect on activity and attention in children.
Quinoline yellow (E 104) (*)	
Carmoisine (E 122) (*)	
Allura red (E 129) (*)	
Tartrazine (E 102) (*)	

Allura red (E 129) (*)	
Tartrazine (E 102) (*)	
Ponceau 4R (E 124) (*)	

(*) ▶M1 With the exception of:
 (a) foods where the colour(s) has been used for the purposes of health or other marking on meat products or for stamping or decorative colouring on eggshells; and
 (b) beverages containing more than 1,2 % by volume of alcohol. ◄

Quinine and caffeine used as a flavouring

Mandatory information on quinine and caffeine used as a flavouring is presented in Regulation (EU) No 1169/2011, link and screenshot accessible below.

http://tiny.cc/mvsrxz

PART D — Designation of flavourings in the list of ingredients

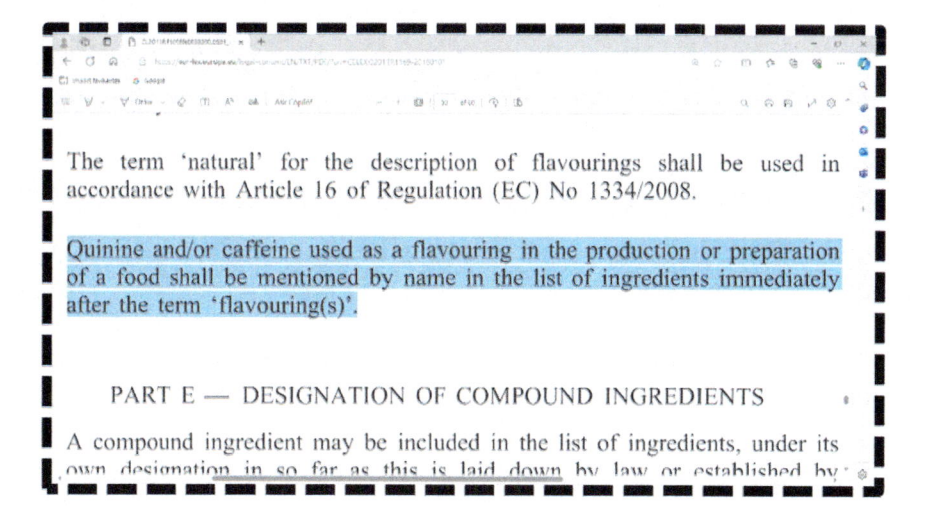

The term 'natural' for the description of flavourings shall be used in accordance with Article 16 of Regulation (EC) No 1334/2008.

Quinine and/or caffeine used as a flavouring in the production or preparation of a food shall be mentioned by name in the list of ingredients immediately after the term 'flavouring(s)'.

PART E — DESIGNATION OF COMPOUND INGREDIENTS

A compound ingredient may be included in the list of ingredients, under its own designation in so far as this is laid down by law or established by

Product or legal name of the food

The name of the food/drink is in essence its legal name. When there is no such name, then the name of the food must be its customary name, or a descriptive name should be adopted if the customary name is not used. A protected trademark, brand name, or fancy name can't be substituted for the name of the food.

The following example illustrates a rum-based beverage with flavourings and sugar added. Let us assume the liquid has a 37.5% alcohol content by volume and 10 g of sugar per litre.

It should be noted that the legal name for this beverage is not "Rum" because you cannot add flavours to rum, and it won't fall under the category of "Liqueur" either since the sugar level is too low. Therefore, it is a "Spirit Drink".

'A spirit drink that does not comply with the requirements laid down for any of the categories of spirit drinks set out in Annex I shall use the legal name "spirit drink".'

If you want to access the definition of rum or spirit drink, you can use the Spirit Regulation 787/2019 for the EU or the Spirit Regulation 110/2008 for the UK, both links below:

http://tiny.cc/qvsrxz

http://tiny.cc/rvsrxz

For the example I have provided above, the word rum could still be used on the label (normally on the front label) to describe the beverage in a more accurate manner. In this case the word rum will be classified as a *compound term*. More information on this can be accessed within the same spirit regulations mentioned above, and you can also use the below guidelines (for EU & for UK) on labelling spirit drinks for further advice:

http://tiny.cc/svsrxz

http://tiny.cc/tvsrxz

As a conclusion, on the back label you would have the legal name "Spirit Drink", whereas on the front label you could have the compound term "Spiced Rum" (if the flavourings used are spices).

Below are more examples of **legal names** for food/drinks:

"Medium mature cheddar cheese, mozzarella and tomato combined with a creamy egg custard encased in a crisp shortcrust pastry"

Or

"Yoghurt coated almonds, peanuts and raisins"

Or

"Mixed Alcoholic Drink with Sweetener"

You have noticed that the above legal name has the word sweetener next to it. This is because if you have a sweetener in your drink/food then this needs to go next to the legal name.

If you have both, sugar and sweetener in, then the legal name will be "Mixed Alcoholic Drink with Sugar and Sweetener."

Note: You can refer to the "Mandatory food information on the label" chapter for guidance on how to label the presence of sweeteners correctly.

How to make an Ingredient list for label purposes

It is normal to list the ingredients on the label in descending order by weight, so you begin with the ingredient with the highest weight and proceed downward. Ingredients constituting less than 2% of the finished product can be listed in a different order after the other ingredients.

It is not necessary to list the amount of the ingredients on the label, unless you are QUID-ing, and I will explain what this means later in the book.

There are a few ingredients that do not require any mention on the label within the Ingredient list section. Examples are: processing aids (e.g., fining agent), carry over additives or substances that serve no technological function in the finished product (e.g., preservative), ingredients that are not present in the final product anymore (e.g., enzyme). It is important to remember that regardless of the role and purpose allergens serve in your food, they must be declared on the label.

In order to list the ingredients on the label, for additives you will have to provide the name of the functional class of that additive, followed by either their name or its E number.

If you would like to find out more about the Ingredient list, please refer to the Regulation (EU) No 1169/2011 and for the UK market you can also access the FSA Guidance, both listed below.

http://tiny.cc/uvsrxz

http://tiny.cc/wvsrxz

An example of an Ingredient list is provided here:

Olive Spread
Water, Olive Oil (22%), Rapeseed Oil, Salt, Emulsifiers (Mono- and Di- Glycerides of Fatty Acids, Sunflower Lecithin), Stabiliser (Sodium Alginate), Preservative (Potassium Sorbate), Acidity Regulator (Lactic Acid), Colour (Beta- Carotene), Natural Flavourings.

Allergens

There are fourteen major allergens that are recognised within the EU, and these are:

1. Cereals containing gluten
2. Crustaceans and products thereof
3. Egg and products thereof
4. Fish and products thereof
5. Peanut and products thereof
6. Soybeans and products thereof
7. Milk and products thereof (including Lactose)
8. Nuts and products thereof
9. Celery and products thereof
10. Mustard and products thereof
11. Sesame seeds and products thereof
12. Sulphur dioxide and sulphites- more than 10 ppm
13. Lupin and products thereof
14. Mollusc and products thereof

Allergens need to be emphasised within the Ingredient list by using a style, font or background colour as a means of distinguishing them from the other ingredients. This also applies to additives, processing aids and any other substances which are present in the final product and are classed as an allergen.

An example of this can be found below:

Sweetened Almond Drink
Water, Sugar (2.5%), **Almonds** (2.3%), Sea Salt, Stabiliser (Gellan Gum), Emulsifier (Sunflower Lecithin).

Substances derived from an allergenic ingredient, which have been highly processed (for example wheat glucose syrup or whey used for making alcoholic distillates), do not need to be declared as allergens because the allergenic material has been removed.

The following links provide more information on allergens (for the UK market):

http://tiny.cc/0wsrxz

http://tiny.cc/1wsrxz

QUID-ing (Quantitative Ingredient Declaration) on ingredients

In a "QUID" declaration, the percentage of an ingredient or category of ingredients is shown. The reason for this is to enable a consumer to make a more informed decision on what to purchase, from similar products on the market.

You should use a QUID declaration in the below examples:

- When a consumer usually associates that ingredient or category of ingredients with that food's name or when it appears in the name of the food;
- When a word, picture, or graphic emphasizes a particular ingredient or ingredient category;
- When, as a result of its name or appearance, an ingredient or group of ingredients is essential for characterizing a food and distinguishing it from other products.

The indication of quantity of an ingredient or category of ingredients is normally given in the form of a percentage % weight/weight. The percentage should normally be calculated by using the same method as that used for determining the order in the list of ingredients. You can use the percentage % volume/volume when it comes to juices. The percentage may be rounded to the nearest whole number, or to the nearest 0.5 decimal place in those cases where it is below 5%.

QUID-ing should appear either in or next to the name of the food or in the Ingredient list.

QUID-ing can be illustrated by the example I gave you previously when discussing "How to make an Ingredient list for label purposes" chapter:

Olive Spread
Water, Olive Oil (22%), Rapeseed Oil, Salt, Emulsifiers (Mono- and Di- Glycerides of Fatty Acids, Sunflower Lecithin), Stabiliser (Sodium

Alginate), Preservative (Potassium Sorbate), Acidity Regulator (Lactic Acid), Colour (Beta- Carotene), Natural Flavourings.

In this case, QUID-ing the olive component is done within the Ingredient list.

As another example, assume you have a Beef Pasty with the following ingredients and quantities:

Ingredients:	Quantity:
Pastry	2 kg
Non- meat ingredients	4.5 kg
Beef	1 kg

In this case when you QUID for beef, you need to consider the weight of the final product after cooking.

Total of weight uncooked is 7.5 kg (2 kg + 4.5 kg + 1 kg)

If we consider that we have 10% loss during cooking, then total of weight after cooking is 6.75 kg.

As a result, you multiply the weight of the beef by 100 and divide it by the total weight of the final product after cooking.

1 * 100 / 6.75 = 14.81%

If we round it up to the nearest whole number, our value will be 15%.

More information on QUID-ing can be found in Article 22 and Annex VIII of the Regulation (EU) No 1169/2011, link listed below.

http://tiny.cc/3wsrxz

Primary Ingredient

A primary ingredient is one that accounts for more than 50% of the food or is associated with the food's name by the consumer and which in most cases requires a quantitative indication.

If the origin of the primary ingredient is different to the origin indication on pack, then you need to label the product with the origin of the primary ingredient.

The primary ingredient is captured in Regulation (EU) No 1169/2011, link and screenshot provided below.

http://tiny.cc/6wsrxz

Article 26 – Country of origin or place of provenance

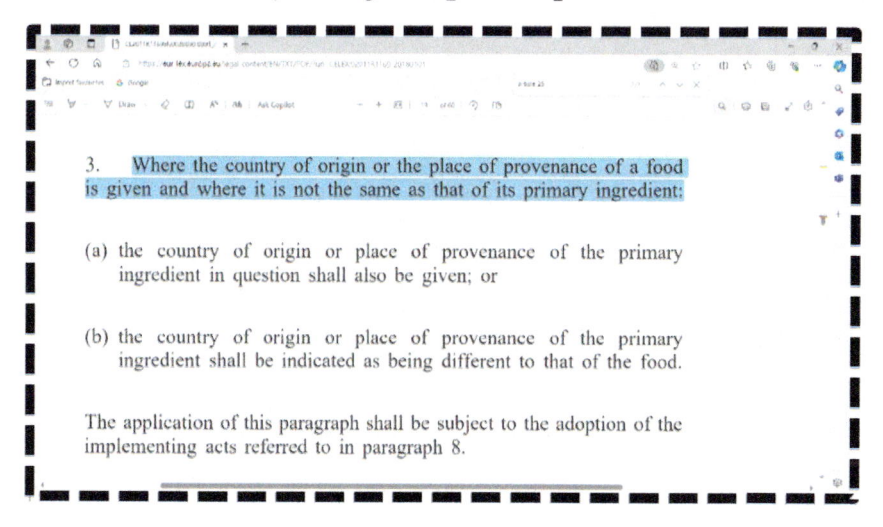

> 3. Where the country of origin or the place of provenance of a food is given and where it is not the same as that of its primary ingredient:
>
> (a) the country of origin or place of provenance of the primary ingredient in question shall also be given; or
>
> (b) the country of origin or place of provenance of the primary ingredient shall be indicated as being different to that of the food.
>
> The application of this paragraph shall be subject to the adoption of the implementing acts referred to in paragraph 8.

List of Additives

Below is a link to the Regulation (EC) No 1333/2008 that includes information on additives -Annex I, as well as screenshots that reference the additive class names.

http://tiny.cc/awsrxz

Additionally, I have included a link to the Food Standards Agency which captures the list of additives approved for use in the UK.

http://tiny.cc/bwsrxz

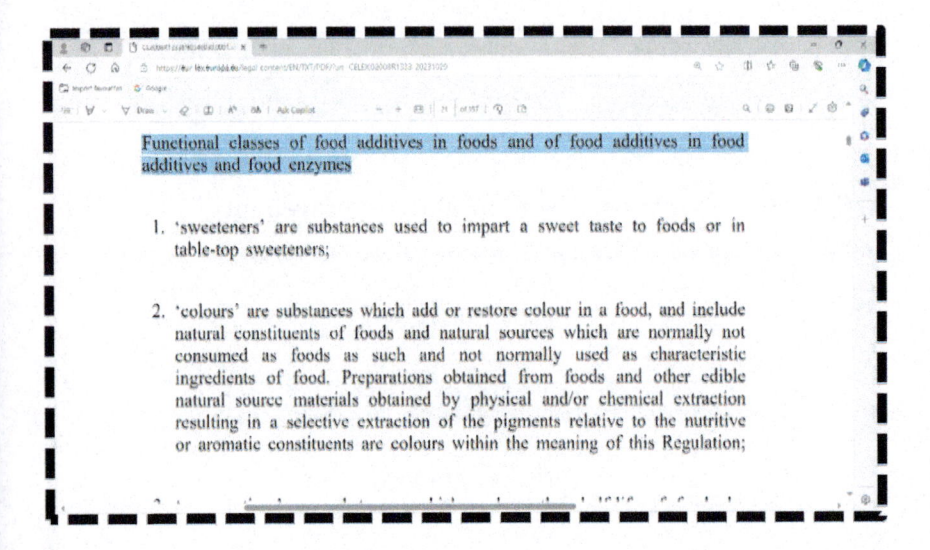

> Functional classes of food additives in foods and of food additives in food additives and food enzymes
>
> 1. 'sweeteners' are substances used to impart a sweet taste to foods or in table-top sweeteners;
>
> 2. 'colours' are substances which add or restore colour in a food, and include natural constituents of foods and natural sources which are normally not consumed as foods as such and not normally used as characteristic ingredients of food. Preparations obtained from foods and other edible natural source materials obtained by physical and/or chemical extraction resulting in a selective extraction of the pigments relative to the nutritive or aromatic constituents are colours within the meaning of this Regulation;

3. 'preservatives' are substances which prolong the shelf-life of foods by protecting them against deterioration caused by micro-organisms and/or which protect against growth of pathogenic micro-organisms;

4. 'antioxidants' are substances which prolong the shelf-life of foods by protecting them against deterioration caused by oxidation, such as fat rancidity and colour changes;

5. 'carriers' are substances used to dissolve, dilute, disperse or otherwise physically modify a food additive or a flavouring, food enzyme, nutrient and/or other substance added for nutritional or physiological purposes to a food without altering its function (and without exerting any technological effect themselves) in order to facilitate its handling, application or use;

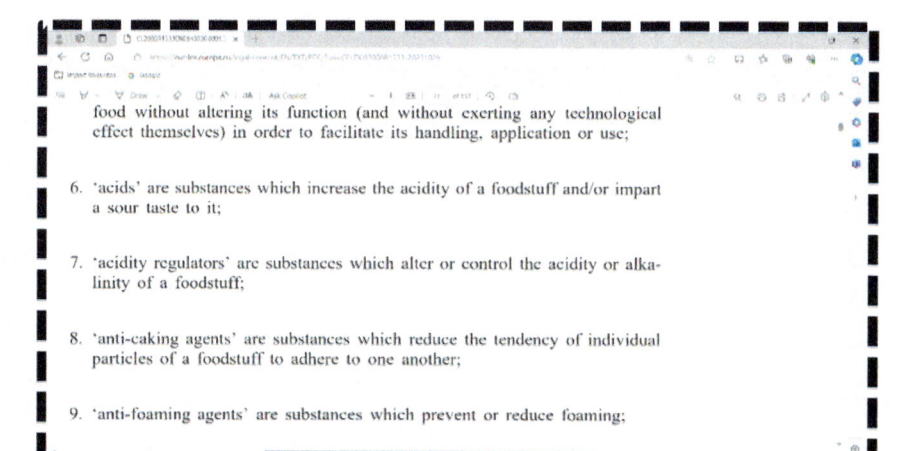

6. 'acids' are substances which increase the acidity of a foodstuff and/or impart a sour taste to it;

7. 'acidity regulators' are substances which alter or control the acidity or alkalinity of a foodstuff;

8. 'anti-caking agents' are substances which reduce the tendency of individual particles of a foodstuff to adhere to one another;

9. 'anti-foaming agents' are substances which prevent or reduce foaming;

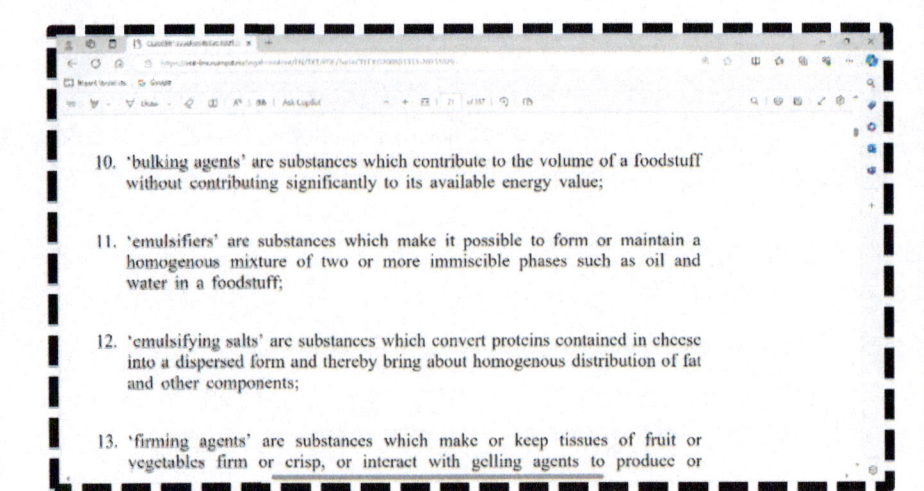

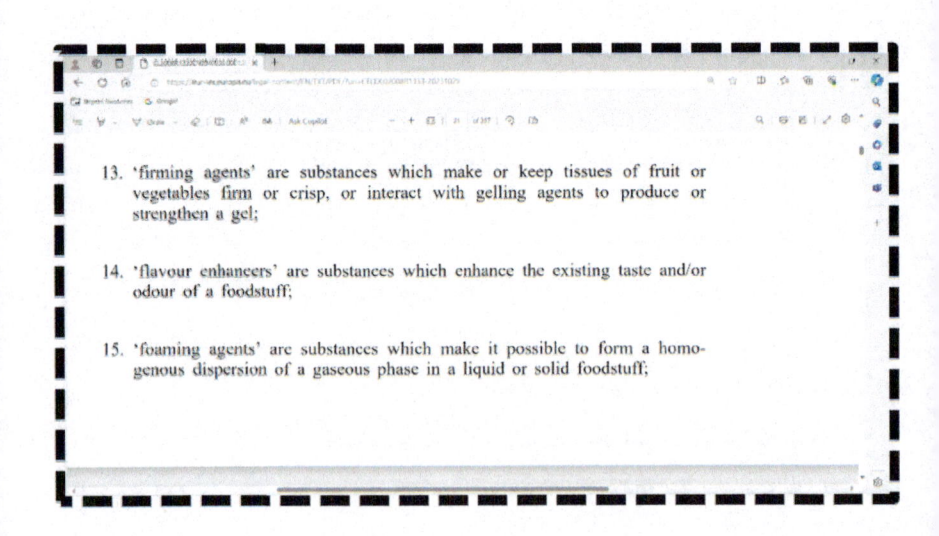

10. 'bulking agents' are substances which contribute to the volume of a foodstuff without contributing significantly to its available energy value;

11. 'emulsifiers' are substances which make it possible to form or maintain a homogenous mixture of two or more immiscible phases such as oil and water in a foodstuff;

12. 'emulsifying salts' are substances which convert proteins contained in cheese into a dispersed form and thereby bring about homogenous distribution of fat and other components;

13. 'firming agents' are substances which make or keep tissues of fruit or vegetables firm or crisp, or interact with gelling agents to produce or strengthen a gel;

14. 'flavour enhancers' are substances which enhance the existing taste and/or odour of a foodstuff;

15. 'foaming agents' are substances which make it possible to form a homogenous dispersion of a gaseous phase in a liquid or solid foodstuff;

16. 'gelling agents' are substances which give a foodstuff texture through formation of a gel;

17. 'glazing agents' (including lubricants) are substances which, when applied to the external surface of a foodstuff, impart a shiny appearance or provide a protective coating;

18. 'humectants' are substances which prevent foods from drying out by counteracting the effect of an atmosphere having a low degree of humidity, or promote the dissolution of a powder in an aqueous medium;

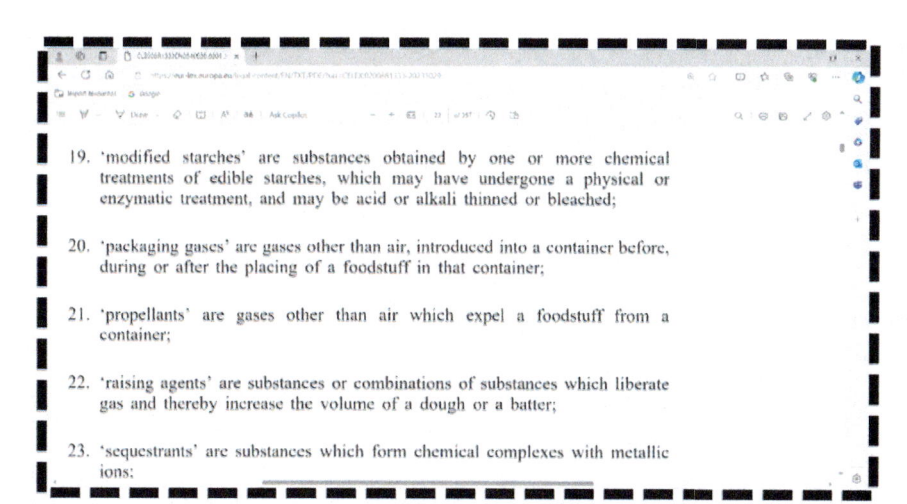

19. 'modified starches' are substances obtained by one or more chemical treatments of edible starches, which may have undergone a physical or enzymatic treatment, and may be acid or alkali thinned or bleached;

20. 'packaging gases' are gases other than air, introduced into a container before, during or after the placing of a foodstuff in that container;

21. 'propellants' are gases other than air which expel a foodstuff from a container;

22. 'raising agents' are substances or combinations of substances which liberate gas and thereby increase the volume of a dough or a batter;

23. 'sequestrants' are substances which form chemical complexes with metallic ions;

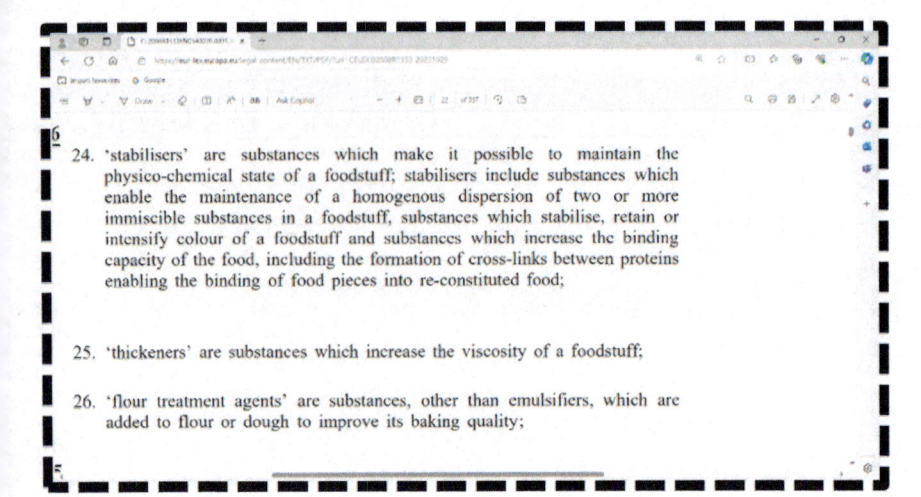

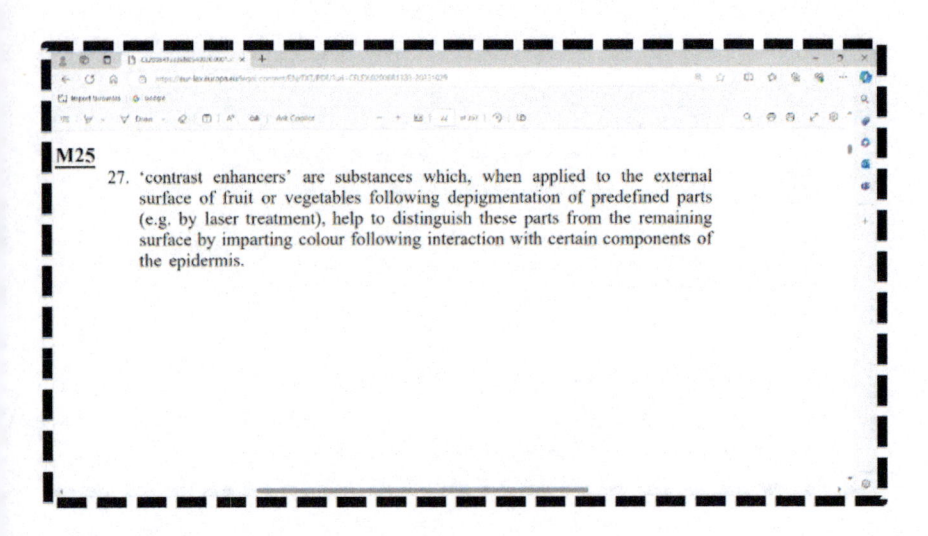

24. 'stabilisers' are substances which make it possible to maintain the physico-chemical state of a foodstuff; stabilisers include substances which enable the maintenance of a homogeneous dispersion of two or more immiscible substances in a foodstuff, substances which stabilise, retain or intensify colour of a foodstuff and substances which increase the binding capacity of the food, including the formation of cross-links between proteins enabling the binding of food pieces into re-constituted food;

25. 'thickeners' are substances which increase the viscosity of a foodstuff;

26. 'flour treatment agents' are substances, other than emulsifiers, which are added to flour or dough to improve its baking quality;

M25
27. 'contrast enhancers' are substances which, when applied to the external surface of fruit or vegetables following depigmentation of predefined parts (e.g. by laser treatment), help to distinguish these parts from the remaining surface by imparting colour following interaction with certain components of the epidermis.

Nutrition declaration

A nutrition declaration on a label must contain certain information that is considered to be mandatory, and this is outlined in Article 30 of Regulation (EU) No 1169/2011.

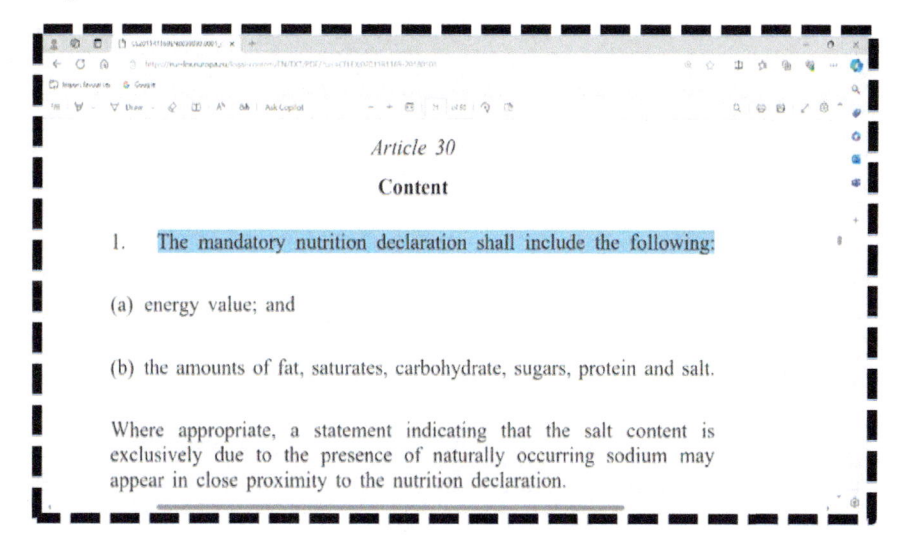

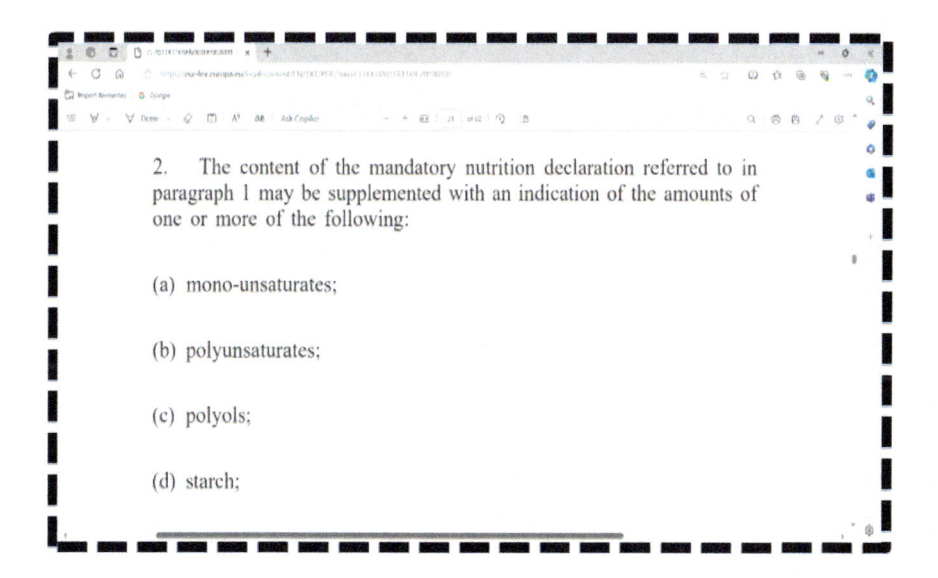

Article 30

Content

1. The mandatory nutrition declaration shall include the following:

(a) energy value; and

(b) the amounts of fat, saturates, carbohydrate, sugars, protein and salt.

Where appropriate, a statement indicating that the salt content is exclusively due to the presence of naturally occurring sodium may appear in close proximity to the nutrition declaration.

2. The content of the mandatory nutrition declaration referred to in paragraph 1 may be supplemented with an indication of the amounts of one or more of the following:

(a) mono-unsaturates;

(b) polyunsaturates;

(c) polyols;

(d) starch;

(e) fibre;

(f) any of the vitamins or minerals listed in point 1 of Part A of Annex XIII, and present in significant amounts as defined in point 2 of Part A of Annex XIII.

3. Where the labelling of a prepacked food provides the mandatory nutrition declaration referred to in paragraph 1, the following information may be repeated thereon:

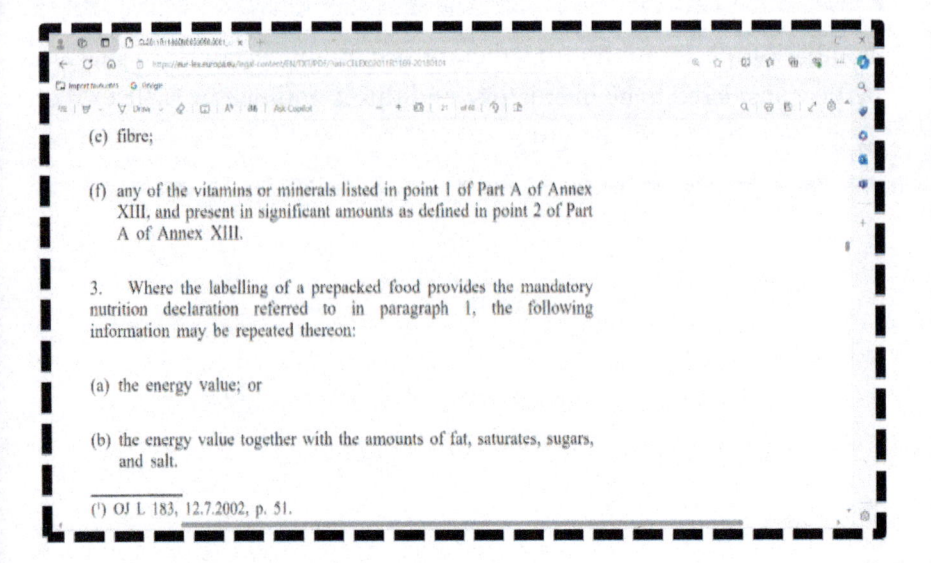

(a) the energy value; or

(b) the energy value together with the amounts of fat, saturates, sugars, and salt.

(¹) OJ L 183, 12.7.2002, p. 51.

In order to calculate the energy value to be declared, the following conversion factors must be used, and these are presented in Annex XIV of Regulation (EU) No 1169/2011.

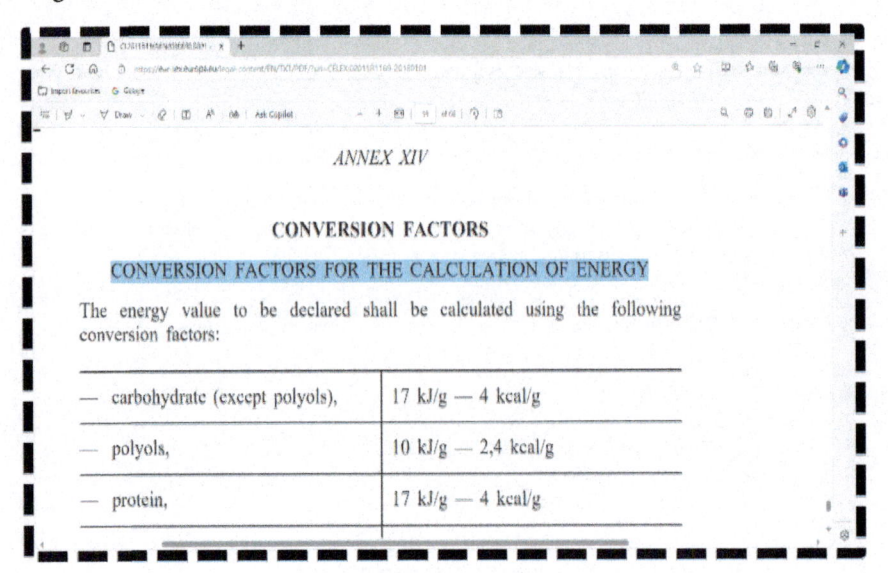

ANNEX XIV

CONVERSION FACTORS

CONVERSION FACTORS FOR THE CALCULATION OF ENERGY

The energy value to be declared shall be calculated using the following conversion factors:

— carbohydrate (except polyols),	17 kJ/g — 4 kcal/g
— polyols,	10 kJ/g — 2,4 kcal/g
— protein,	17 kJ/g — 4 kcal/g

— fat,	37 kJ/g — 9 kcal/g
— salatrims,	25 kJ/g — 6 kcal/g
— alcohol (ethanol),	29 kJ/g — 7 kcal/g
— organic acid,	13 kJ/g — 3 kcal/g
— fibre,	8 kJ/g — 2 kcal/g
— erythritol,	0 kJ/g — 0 kcal/g

The units of measurement used in the nutrition declaration, as well as the order in which the information is presented, are captured in Annex XV of Regulation (EU) No 1169/2011, screenshots provided below:

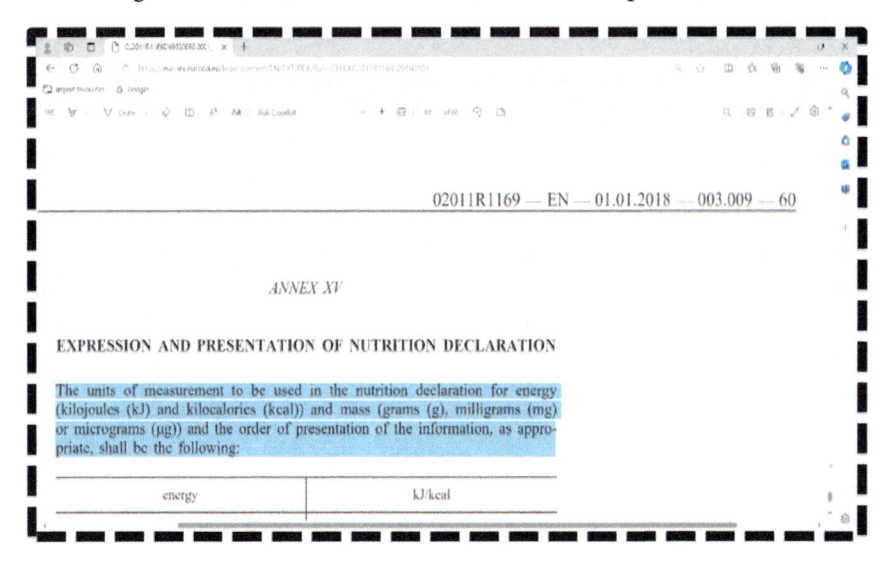

02011R1169 — EN — 01.01.2018 — 003.009 — 60

ANNEX XV

EXPRESSION AND PRESENTATION OF NUTRITION DECLARATION

The units of measurement to be used in the nutrition declaration for energy (kilojoules (kJ) and kilocalories (kcal)) and mass (grams (g), milligrams (mg) or micrograms (μg)) and the order of presentation of the information, as appropriate, shall be the following:

energy	kJ/kcal

energy	kJ/kcal
fat	g
of which	
— saturates,	g
— mono-unsaturates,	g
— polyunsaturates,	g

— polyunsaturates,	g
carbohydrate	g
of which	
— sugars,	g
— polyols,	g
— starch,	g
fibre	g

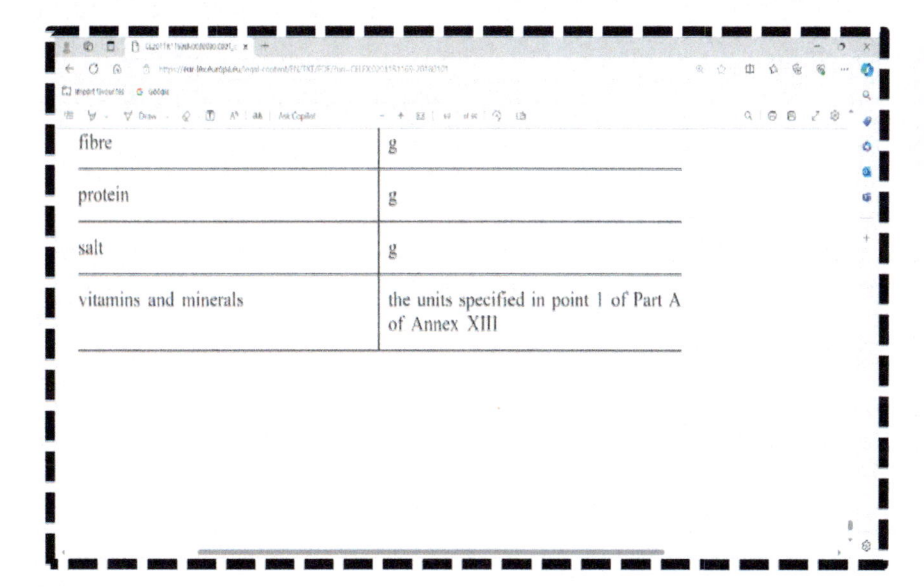

fibre	g
protein	g
salt	g
vitamins and minerals	the units specified in point 1 of Part A of Annex XIII

Along with the screenshots above, I have also added a link to Regulation (EU) No 1169/2011.

http://tiny.cc/dwsrxz

Nutrition claims

Nutrition claims and conditions applying to them are captured in the Annex of Regulation (EC) No 1924/2006 on nutrition and health claims made on foods, link and screenshots provided below:

http://tiny.cc/gwsrxz

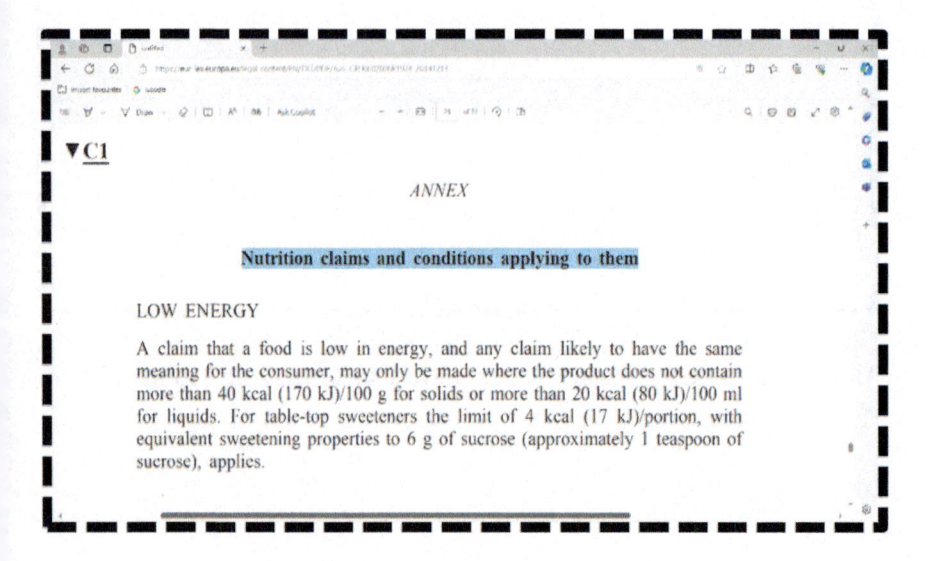

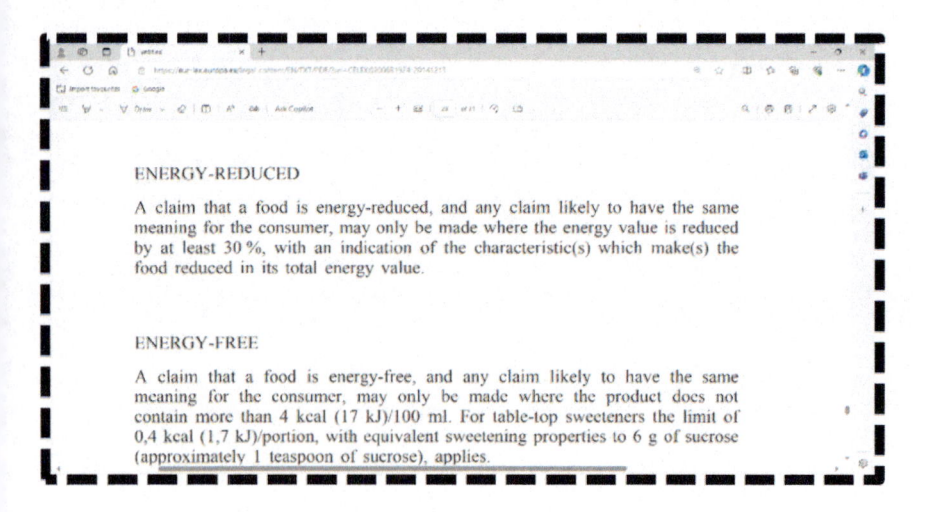

> **ANNEX**
>
> **Nutrition claims and conditions applying to them**
>
> LOW ENERGY
>
> A claim that a food is low in energy, and any claim likely to have the same meaning for the consumer, may only be made where the product does not contain more than 40 kcal (170 kJ)/100 g for solids or more than 20 kcal (80 kJ)/100 ml for liquids. For table-top sweeteners the limit of 4 kcal (17 kJ)/portion, with equivalent sweetening properties to 6 g of sucrose (approximately 1 teaspoon of sucrose), applies.

> ENERGY-REDUCED
>
> A claim that a food is energy-reduced, and any claim likely to have the same meaning for the consumer, may only be made where the energy value is reduced by at least 30 %, with an indication of the characteristic(s) which make(s) the food reduced in its total energy value.
>
> ENERGY-FREE
>
> A claim that a food is energy-free, and any claim likely to have the same meaning for the consumer, may only be made where the product does not contain more than 4 kcal (17 kJ)/100 ml. For table-top sweeteners the limit of 0,4 kcal (1,7 kJ)/portion, with equivalent sweetening properties to 6 g of sucrose (approximately 1 teaspoon of sucrose), applies.

LOW FAT

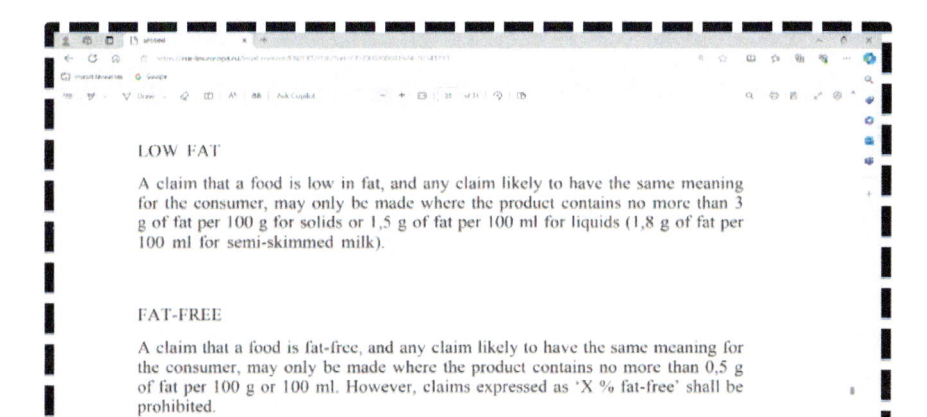

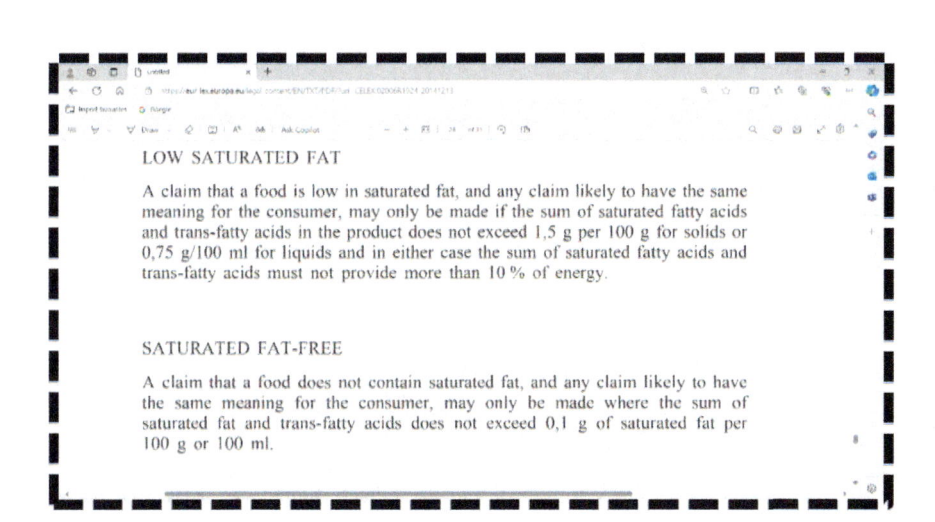

A claim that a food is low in fat, and any claim likely to have the same meaning for the consumer, may only be made where the product contains no more than 3 g of fat per 100 g for solids or 1,5 g of fat per 100 ml for liquids (1,8 g of fat per 100 ml for semi-skimmed milk).

FAT-FREE

A claim that a food is fat-free, and any claim likely to have the same meaning for the consumer, may only be made where the product contains no more than 0,5 g of fat per 100 g or 100 ml. However, claims expressed as 'X % fat-free' shall be prohibited.

LOW SATURATED FAT

A claim that a food is low in saturated fat, and any claim likely to have the same meaning for the consumer, may only be made if the sum of saturated fatty acids and trans-fatty acids in the product does not exceed 1,5 g per 100 g for solids or 0,75 g/100 ml for liquids and in either case the sum of saturated fatty acids and trans-fatty acids must not provide more than 10 % of energy.

SATURATED FAT-FREE

A claim that a food does not contain saturated fat, and any claim likely to have the same meaning for the consumer, may only be made where the sum of saturated fat and trans-fatty acids does not exceed 0,1 g of saturated fat per 100 g or 100 ml.

LOW SUGARS

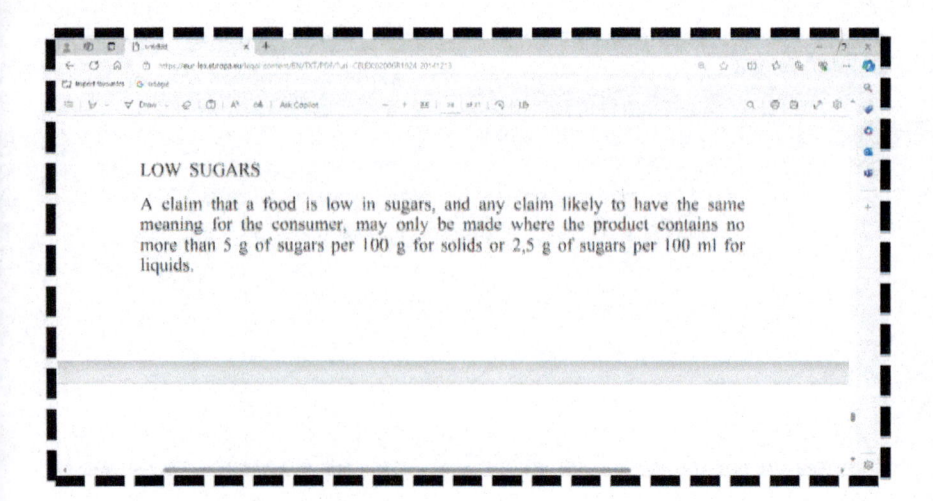

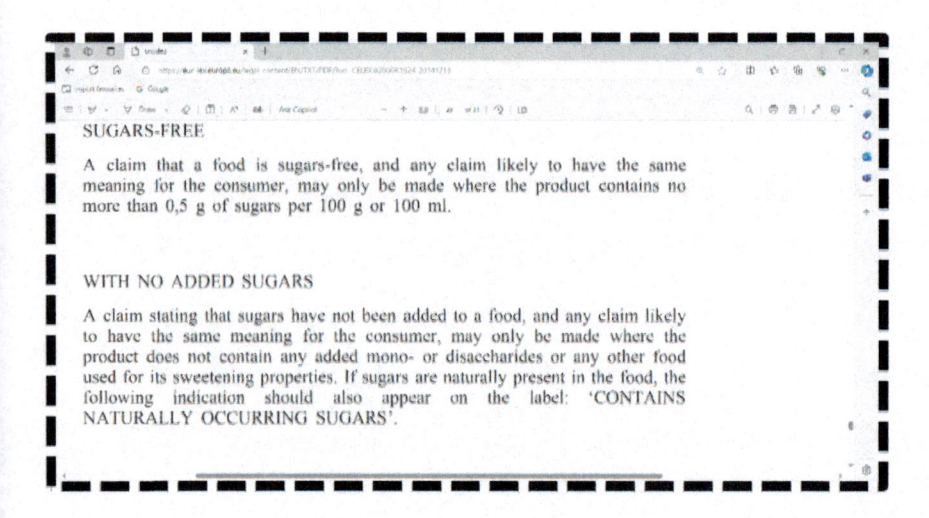

A claim that a food is low in sugars, and any claim likely to have the same meaning for the consumer, may only be made where the product contains no more than 5 g of sugars per 100 g for solids or 2,5 g of sugars per 100 ml for liquids.

SUGARS-FREE

A claim that a food is sugars-free, and any claim likely to have the same meaning for the consumer, may only be made where the product contains no more than 0,5 g of sugars per 100 g or 100 ml.

WITH NO ADDED SUGARS

A claim stating that sugars have not been added to a food, and any claim likely to have the same meaning for the consumer, may only be made where the product does not contain any added mono- or disaccharides or any other food used for its sweetening properties. If sugars are naturally present in the food, the following indication should also appear on the label: 'CONTAINS NATURALLY OCCURRING SUGARS'.

LOW SODIUM/SALT

A claim that a food is low in sodium/salt, and any claim likely to have the same meaning for the consumer, may only be made where the product contains no more than 0,12 g of sodium, or the equivalent value for salt, per 100 g or per 100 ml. For waters, other than natural mineral waters falling within the scope of Directive 80/777/EEC, this value should not exceed 2 mg of sodium per 100 ml.

VERY LOW SODIUM/SALT

A claim that a food is very low in sodium/salt, and any claim likely to have the same meaning for the consumer, may only be made where the product contains no more than 0,04 g of sodium, or the equivalent value for salt, per 100 g or per 100 ml. This claim shall not be used for natural mineral waters and other waters.

SODIUM-FREE or SALT-FREE

A claim that a food is sodium-free or salt-free, and any claim likely to have the same meaning for the consumer, may only be made where the product contains no more than 0,005 g of sodium, or the equivalent value for salt, per 100 g.

▼ M5

NO ADDED SODIUM/SALT

A claim stating that sodium/salt has not been added to a food and any claim likely to have the same meaning for the consumer may only be made where the product does not contain any added sodium/salt or any other ingredient containing added sodium/salt and the product contains no more than 0,12 g sodium, or the equivalent value for salt, per 100 g or 100 ml.

SOURCE OF FIBRE

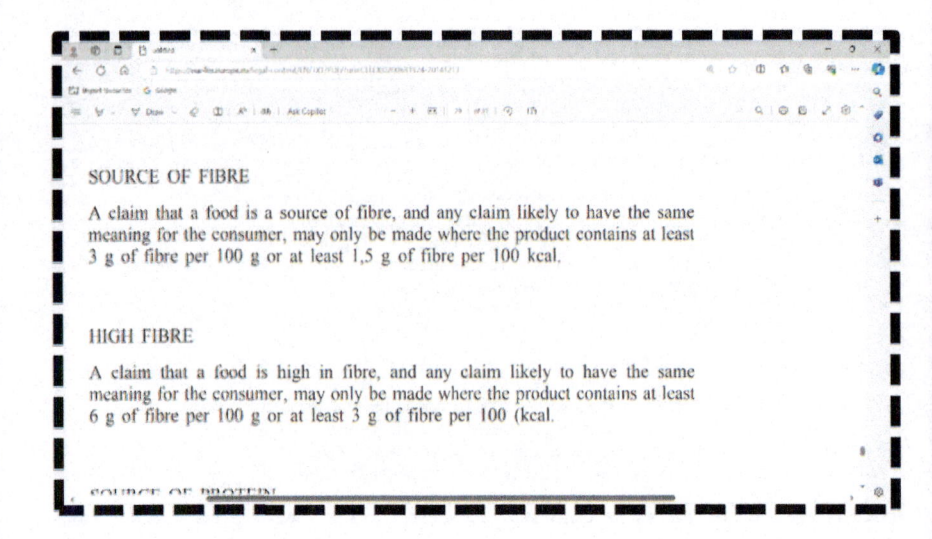

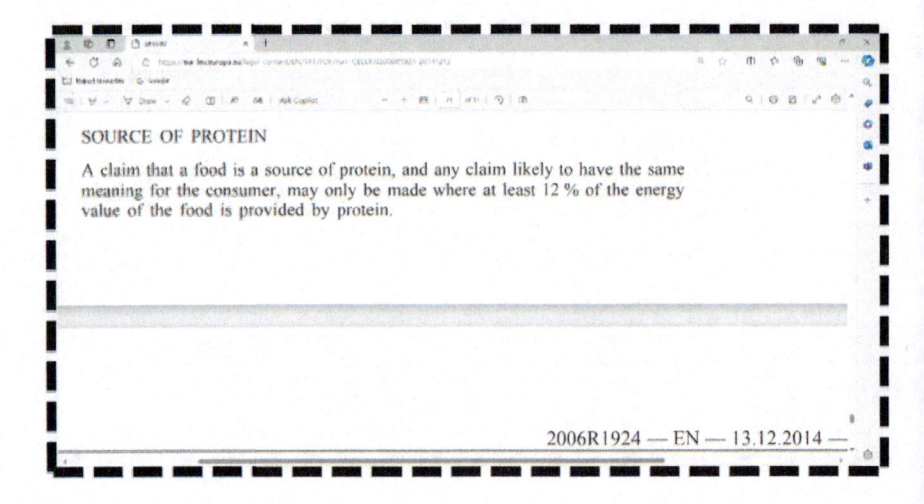

A claim that a food is a source of fibre, and any claim likely to have the same meaning for the consumer, may only be made where the product contains at least 3 g of fibre per 100 g or at least 1,5 g of fibre per 100 kcal.

HIGH FIBRE

A claim that a food is high in fibre, and any claim likely to have the same meaning for the consumer, may only be made where the product contains at least 6 g of fibre per 100 g or at least 3 g of fibre per 100 (kcal.

SOURCE OF PROTEIN

A claim that a food is a source of protein, and any claim likely to have the same meaning for the consumer, may only be made where at least 12 % of the energy value of the food is provided by protein.

2006R1924 — EN — 13.12.2014

HIGH PROTEIN

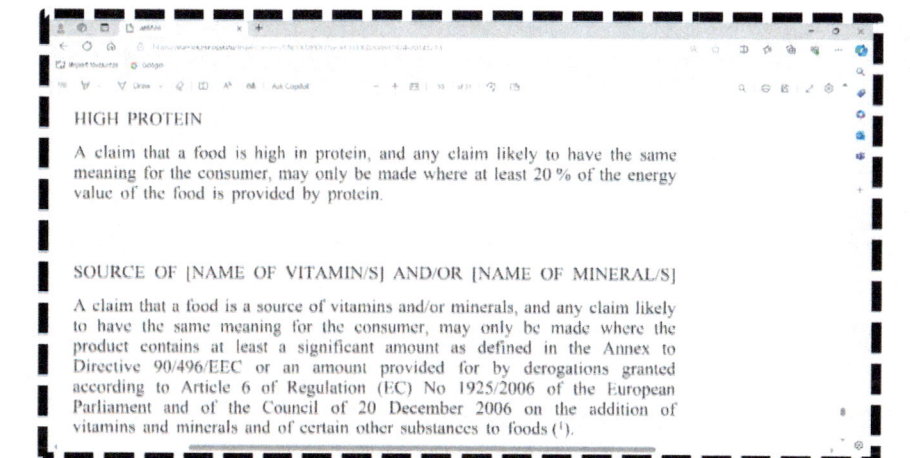

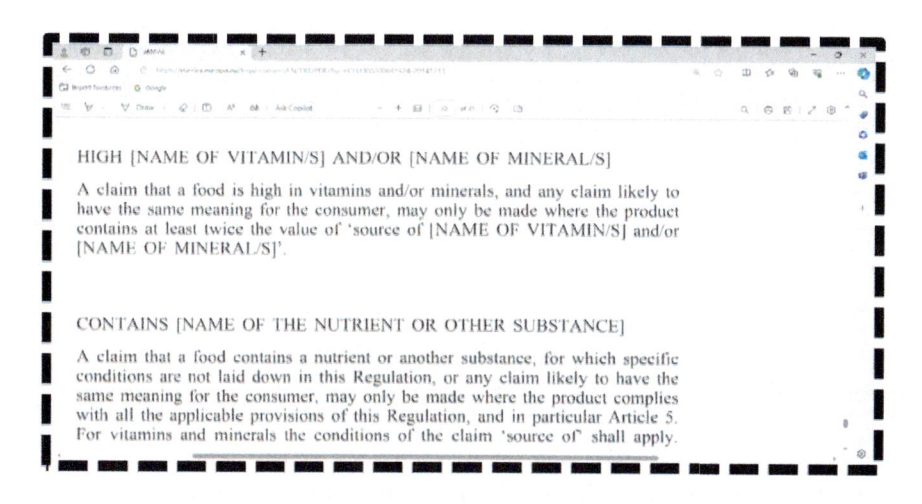

A claim that a food is high in protein, and any claim likely to have the same meaning for the consumer, may only be made where at least 20 % of the energy value of the food is provided by protein.

SOURCE OF [NAME OF VITAMIN/S] AND/OR [NAME OF MINERAL/S]

A claim that a food is a source of vitamins and/or minerals, and any claim likely to have the same meaning for the consumer, may only be made where the product contains at least a significant amount as defined in the Annex to Directive 90/496/EEC or an amount provided for by derogations granted according to Article 6 of Regulation (EC) No 1925/2006 of the European Parliament and of the Council of 20 December 2006 on the addition of vitamins and minerals and of certain other substances to foods ([1]).

HIGH [NAME OF VITAMIN/S] AND/OR [NAME OF MINERAL/S]

A claim that a food is high in vitamins and/or minerals, and any claim likely to have the same meaning for the consumer, may only be made where the product contains at least twice the value of 'source of [NAME OF VITAMIN/S] and/or [NAME OF MINERAL/S]'.

CONTAINS [NAME OF THE NUTRIENT OR OTHER SUBSTANCE]

A claim that a food contains a nutrient or another substance, for which specific conditions are not laid down in this Regulation, or any claim likely to have the same meaning for the consumer, may only be made where the product complies with all the applicable provisions of this Regulation, and in particular Article 5. For vitamins and minerals the conditions of the claim 'source of' shall apply.

same meaning for the consumer, may only be made where the product complies with all the applicable provisions of this Regulation, and in particular Article 5. For vitamins and minerals the conditions of the claim 'source of' shall apply.

INCREASED [NAME OF THE NUTRIENT]

A claim stating that the content in one or more nutrients, other than vitamins and minerals, has been increased, and any claim likely to have the same meaning for the consumer, may only be made where the product meets the conditions for the claim 'source of' and the increase in content is at least 30 % compared to a similar product.

REDUCED [NAME OF THE NUTRIENT]

---

minerals, has been increased, and any claim likely to have the same meaning for the consumer, may only be made where the product meets the conditions for the claim 'source of' and the increase in content is at least 30 % compared to a similar product.

REDUCED [NAME OF THE NUTRIENT]

A claim stating that the content in one or more nutrients has been reduced, and any claim likely to have the same meaning for the consumer, may only be made where the reduction in content is at least 30 % compared to a similar product, except for micronutrients, where a 10 % difference in the reference values as set in Directive 90/496/EEC shall be acceptable, and for sodium, or the equivalent value for salt, where a 25 % difference shall be acceptable.

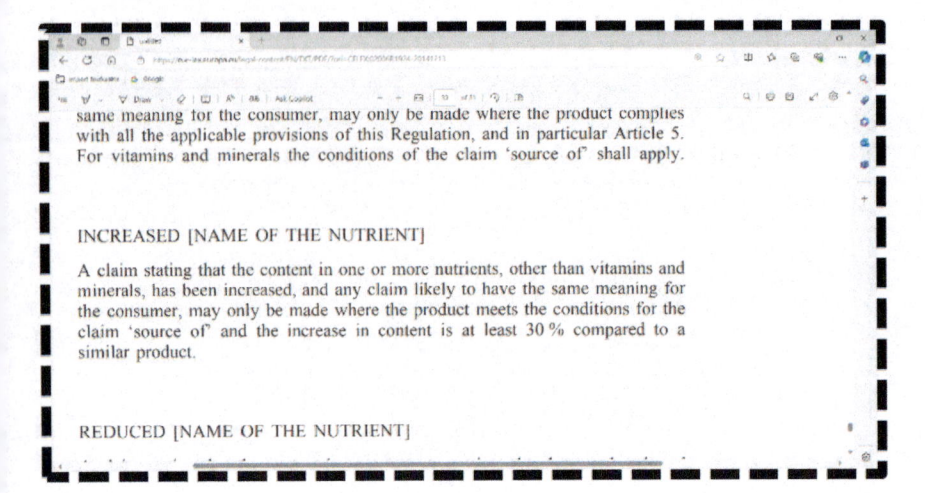

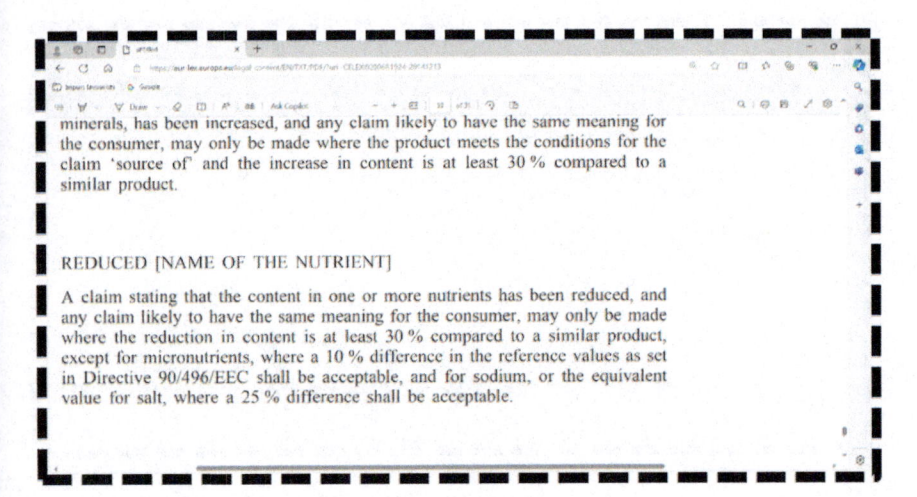

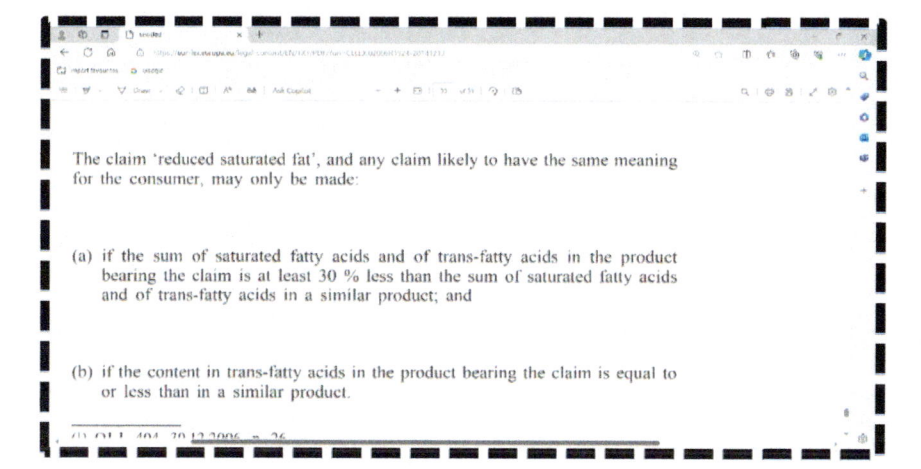

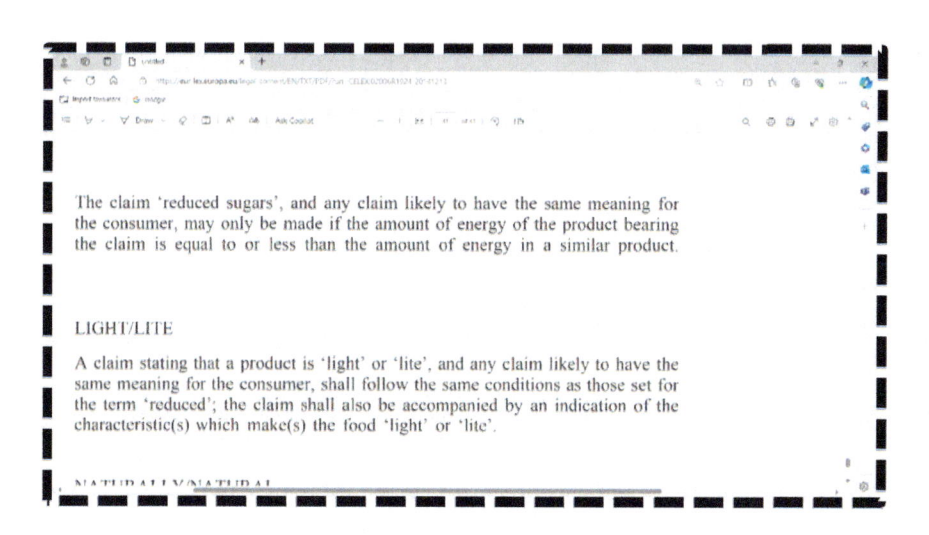

The claim 'reduced saturated fat', and any claim likely to have the same meaning for the consumer, may only be made:

(a) if the sum of saturated fatty acids and of trans-fatty acids in the product bearing the claim is at least 30 % less than the sum of saturated fatty acids and of trans-fatty acids in a similar product; and

(b) if the content in trans-fatty acids in the product bearing the claim is equal to or less than in a similar product.

The claim 'reduced sugars', and any claim likely to have the same meaning for the consumer, may only be made if the amount of energy of the product bearing the claim is equal to or less than the amount of energy in a similar product.

LIGHT/LITE

A claim stating that a product is 'light' or 'lite', and any claim likely to have the same meaning for the consumer, shall follow the same conditions as those set for the term 'reduced'; the claim shall also be accompanied by an indication of the characteristic(s) which make(s) the food 'light' or 'lite'.

NATURALLY/NATURAL

NATURALLY/NATURAL

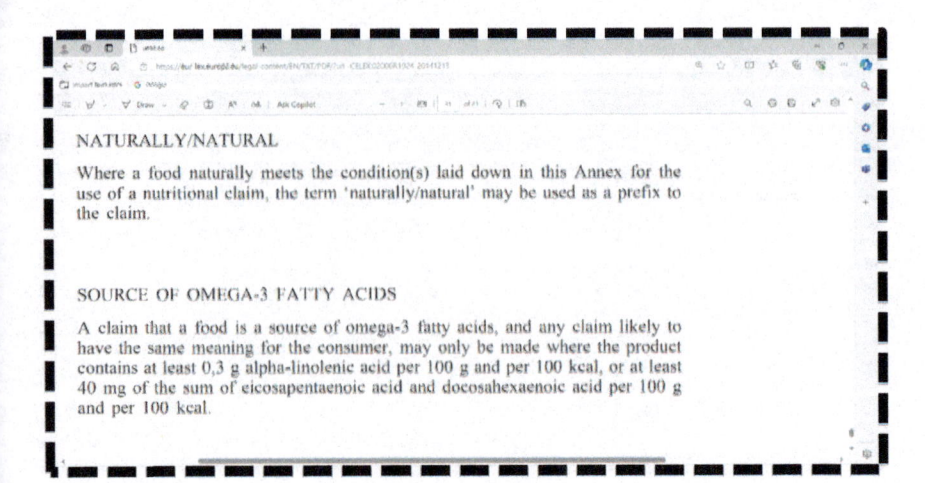

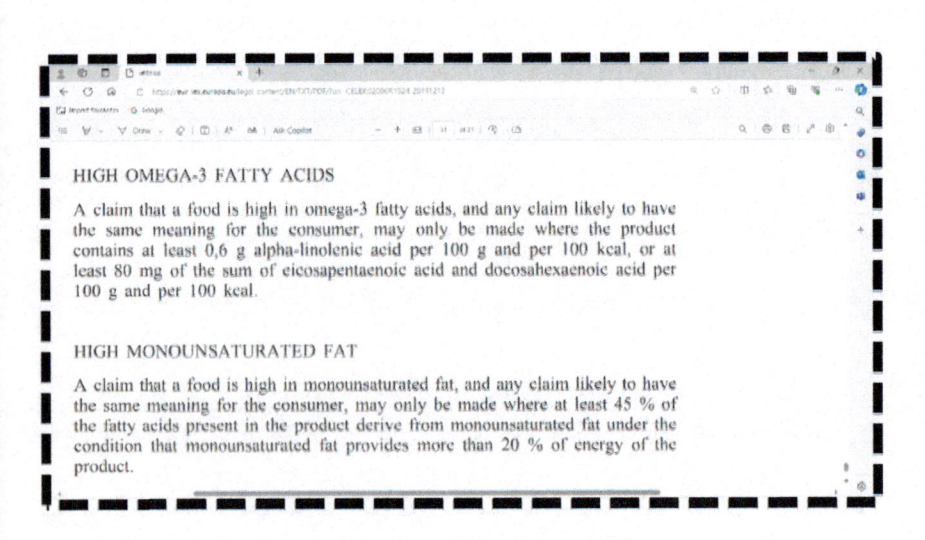

Where a food naturally meets the condition(s) laid down in this Annex for the use of a nutritional claim, the term 'naturally/natural' may be used as a prefix to the claim.

SOURCE OF OMEGA-3 FATTY ACIDS

A claim that a food is a source of omega-3 fatty acids, and any claim likely to have the same meaning for the consumer, may only be made where the product contains at least 0,3 g alpha-linolenic acid per 100 g and per 100 kcal, or at least 40 mg of the sum of eicosapentaenoic acid and docosahexaenoic acid per 100 g and per 100 kcal.

HIGH OMEGA-3 FATTY ACIDS

A claim that a food is high in omega-3 fatty acids, and any claim likely to have the same meaning for the consumer, may only be made where the product contains at least 0,6 g alpha-linolenic acid per 100 g and per 100 kcal, or at least 80 mg of the sum of eicosapentaenoic acid and docosahexaenoic acid per 100 g and per 100 kcal.

HIGH MONOUNSATURATED FAT

A claim that a food is high in monounsaturated fat, and any claim likely to have the same meaning for the consumer, may only be made where at least 45 % of the fatty acids present in the product derive from monounsaturated fat under the condition that monounsaturated fat provides more than 20 % of energy of the product.

HIGH POLYUNSATURATED FAT

A claim that a food is high in polyunsaturated fat, and any claim likely to have the same meaning for the consumer, may only be made where at least 45 % of the fatty acids present in the product derive from polyunsaturated fat under the condition that polyunsaturated fat provides more than 20 % of energy of the product.

HIGH UNSATURATED FAT

A claim that a food is high in unsaturated fat, and any claim likely to have the same meaning for the consumer may only be made where at least 70 % of the fatty acids present in the product derive from unsaturated fat under the condition that unsaturated fat provides more than 20 % of energy of the product.

Guidance on the use of the terms natural, pure, traditional etc.

"**Natural**" refers to a product that contains natural ingredients, e.g., ingredients that have been produced by nature, without human intervention.

Usually, the term "**pure**" refers to single ingredient foods or to food with high-quality ingredients.

"**Original**" is used to indicate a product that was the first of its kind to enter the market, where the original form or taste has remained essentially unchanged, and thus to distinguish it from new products within the range.

"**Traditional**" often refers to a product or a method of preparation when there are newer alternatives available.

The term "**authentic**", "**real**" and "**genuine**" may refer to a product that has remained unchanged throughout time, or to a product that originates from the area suggested by its name when the generic description has become more widely used.

"**Fresh**" produce is generally considered to have been harvested or manufactured relatively recently. It can also refer to unprocessed products.

In the consumer's mind, "**home-made**" means food that has been prepared in a household kitchen rather than in a factory or manufacturing facility.

The term "**hand-made**" should refer to a product whose majority of the process is done by hand rather than just one element.

Below, I have included a link from the Food Standards Agency that provides more information on these kinds of terms.

http://tiny.cc/iwsrxz

Steviol Glycosides

Steviol glycosides are compounds extracted from the stevia plant and they act as sweeteners. While they all have the same chemical foundation, they differ from one another in terms of their final configuration. To translate from one form to another, you can refer to their molar mass which I have captured below. The base structure for all steviol glycosides is steviol.

Steviol Glycoside	Molar Mass
Steviol	318.45
Stevioside	804.87
Rebaudioside A	967.01
Rebaudioside B	804.88
Rebaudioside C	951.01
Rebaudioside D	1129.15
Rebaudioside E	967.01
Rebaudioside F	936.90
Rebaudioside M	1291.29
Dulcoside A	788.87
Rubusoside	642.73
Steviolbioside	642.73

In the EU, steviol glycosides are regulated in terms of dosage and they are expressed here as steviol equivalents. I have included a link below to Regulation (EU) No 1131/2011 that you might find helpful.

http://tiny.cc/mwsrxz

To illustrate, if you wish to develop a product containing 182 mg/L of Rebaudioside A and want to convert it into steviol equivalents, then you would do the following:

182 * 318.45 / 967.01 = 60 mg/L of steviol equivalents

Enzymes: what are they

Enzymes are biomacromolecules which by decreasing the activation energy they increase the speed of the reaction. In other words, they are biological catalysts which accelerate a chemical reaction.

Enzymes are very much dependent on temperature and ph (among other factors), meaning that they work best within a specific range and do not work at all out of these parameters.

There are a variety of enzymes available, each acting on a so-called substrate. The following are some examples of enzymes and the substrates they act on:

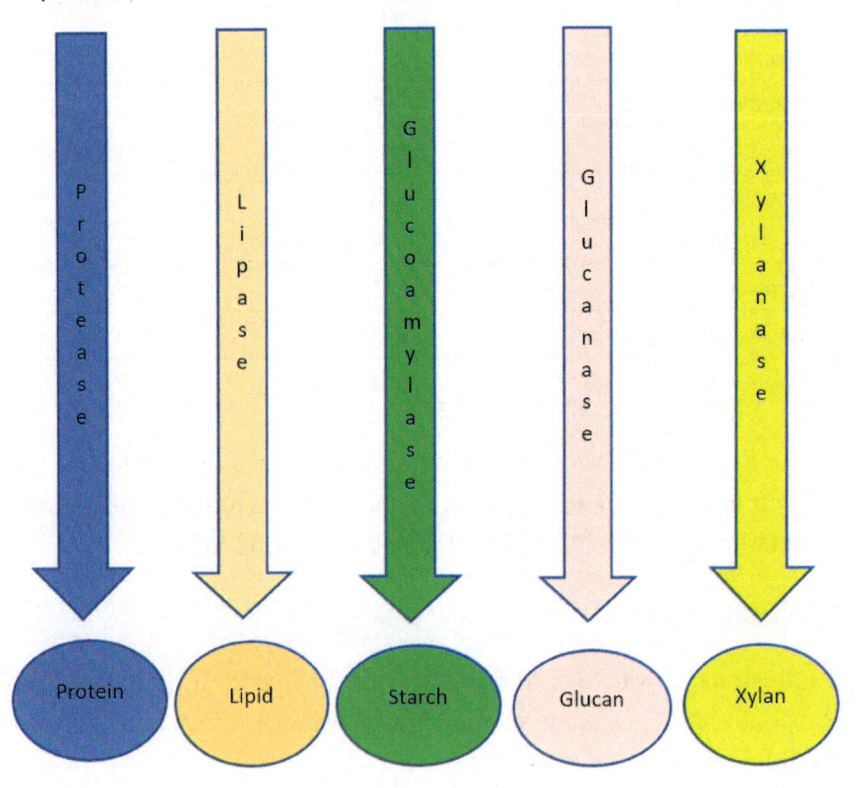

Protease	Lipase	Glucoamylase	Glucanase	Xylanase
Protein	Lipid	Starch	Glucan	Xylan

Next, I will illustrate how enzymes interact with a substrate and provide an example from a flour batch that was used in the making of biscuits. During this process, an alveograph test was performed to determine the baking potential of the flour.

Legend:

W = the amount of energy required to deform the dough into a bubble until it ruptures

L = flexibility of the dough without breaking

P = dough's resistance to deformation when stretched

As can be seen in the graph below, **amylase** and **protease,** used together in this test, significantly improved the flour, which made it easier to work with during our application–making biscuits.

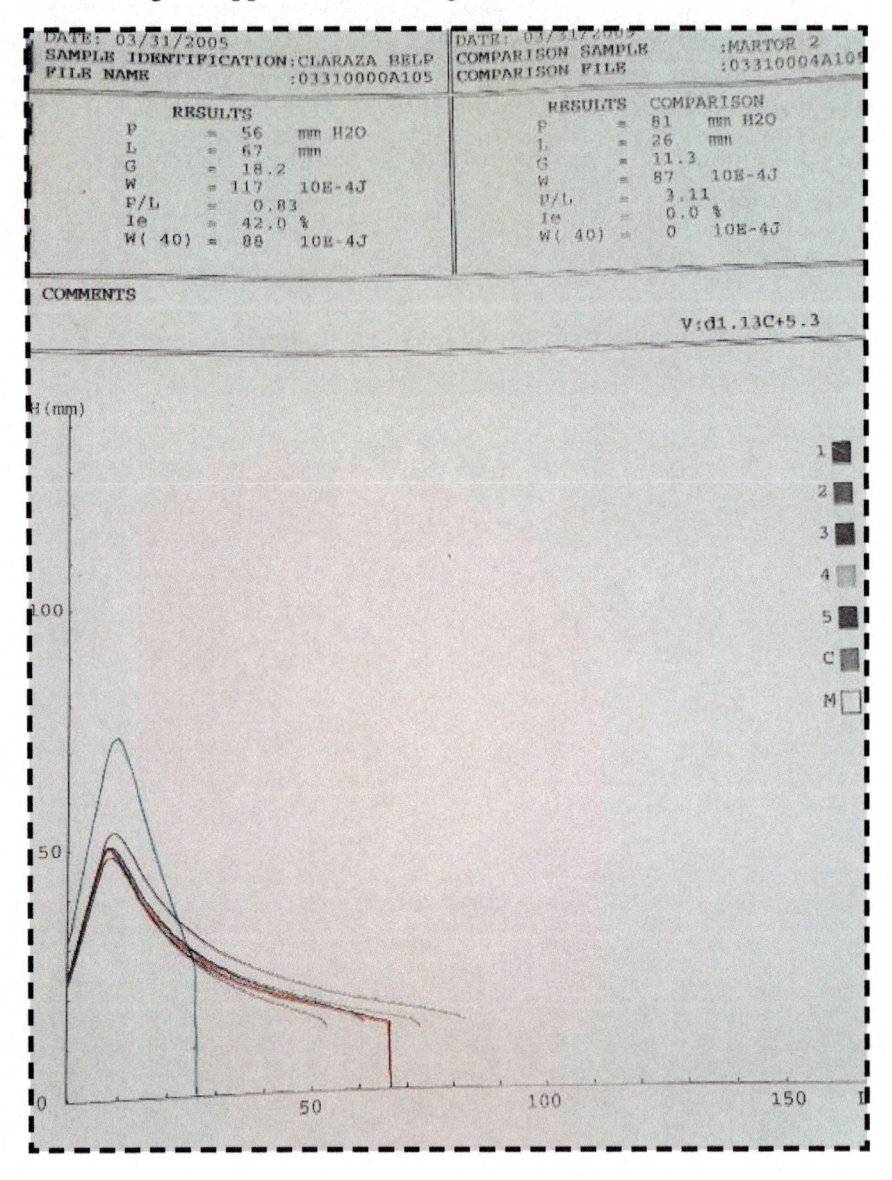

Using **hemicellulase** in this test has not improved the quality of the flour for our application–making biscuits.

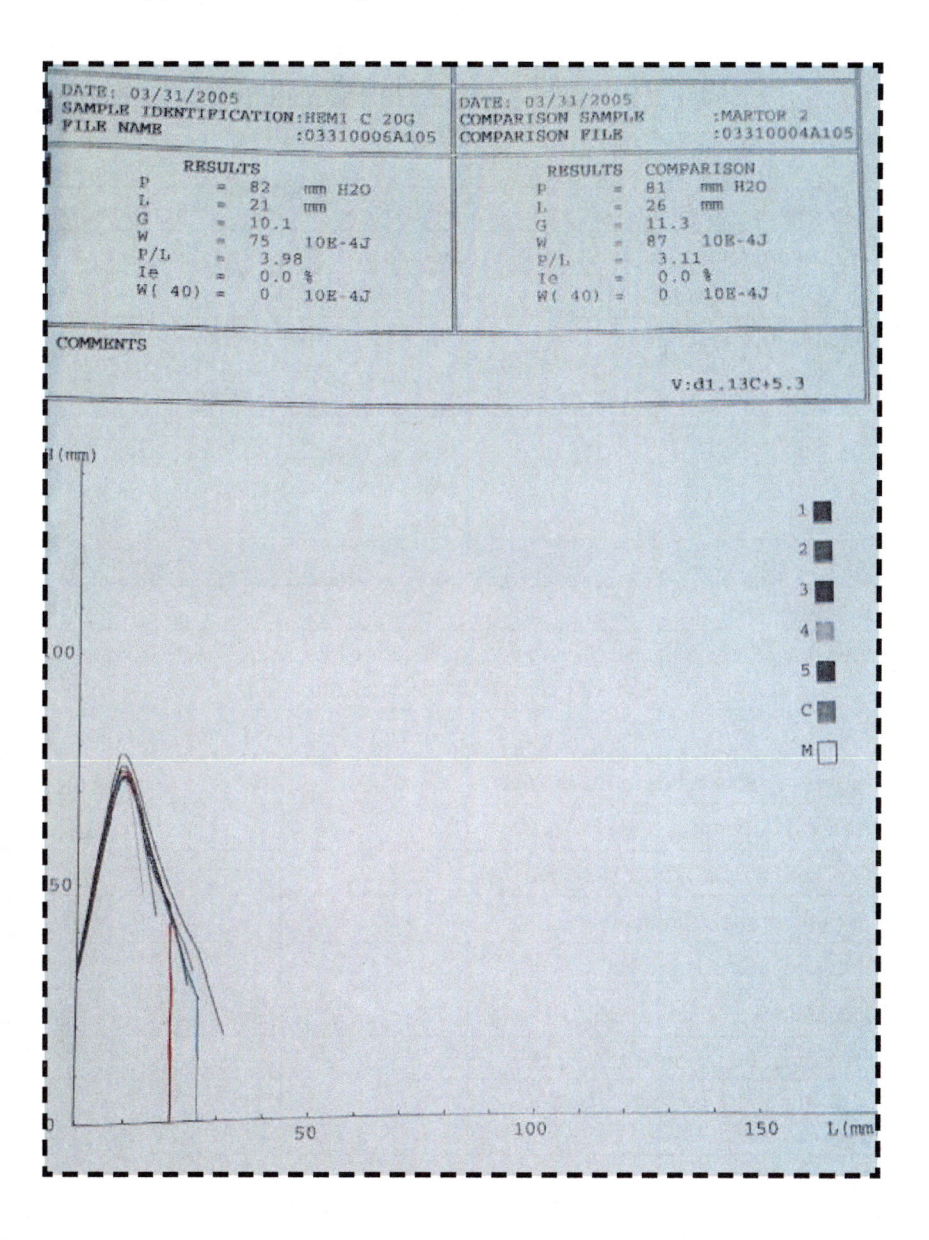

How to make a final Product Specification

The following example illustrates how information can be provided about a product, including an organoleptic description, a list of ingredients, information about allergen status, diet suitability and nutritional information.

Name of the product	Pink Grapefruit & Melon Beverage
Type of product	Soft Drink
Internal reference code	R111298
Organoleptic description	Nose – A zesty grapefruit scent accompanied by a sweet melon aroma. Palate – Grapefruit taste with a good balance between bitterness, acidity and fruitiness, finishing with a juicy melon note.

Ingredient list

Carbonated Water, Sugar, Flavourings, Acidifier (Citric Acid), Preservatives (Potassium Sorbate, Sodium Benzoate), Colour (Anthocyanin).

Presence of allergens in the product	Yes	No
Cereals containing gluten		✓
Crustaceans and products thereof		✓
Egg and products thereof		✓
Fish and products thereof		✓
Peanut and products thereof		✓
Soybeans and products thereof		✓
Milk and products thereof (including Lactose)		✓
Nuts and products thereof		✓
Celery and products thereof		✓
Mustard and products thereof		✓
Sesame seeds and products thereof		✓

Sulphur dioxide and sulphites		✓
Lupin and products thereof		✓
Mollusc and products thereof		✓

Diet suitability	Yes	No
Vegetarian	✓	
Ovo-lacto vegetarian	✓	
Vegan	✓	
Kosher	Suitable, not certified	
Halal		✓
Coeliac	✓	
Lactose intolerant	✓	

Nutritional information (average values)	
Energy	29 kJ / 123 kcal
Fat	0 g
of which	
Saturates	0 g
Carbohydrate	7.0 g
of which	
Sugars	7.0 g
Protein	0 g
Salt	0 g

Section 3: – Management level

How to determine if a particular EU Regulation is still in force

To determine whether a particular legislation is still in force, you will need to use the EUR-Lex page as this is the official search engine that can assist you with finding the most up-to-date European Regulation.

If, for example, you would like to access Regulation (EU) No 1169/2011 on the provision of food information to consumers, then you would enter *32011R1169* in the QUICK SEARCH field.

32011R1169 is the so-called CELEX number, where 2011 makes reference to the year when this Regulation was first published, and 1169 refers to its actual number, to distinguish it from other Regulations.

If the Regulation you are searching for has only three digits within its number instead of four, then you will need to add 0 (zero) at the beginning of your number.

Following completion of the above step, you will need to click on the date that appears next to Current consolidated version: 01/01/2018. The reason for this is so that you can use the most recent version of that Regulation. To illustrate this, please see below:

Regulation (EU) No 1169/2011 of the European Parliament and of the Council of 25 October 2011 on the provision of food information to consumers, amending Regulations (EC) No 1924/2006 and (EC) No 1925/2006 of the European Parliament and of the Council, and repealing Commission Directive 87/250/EEC, Council Directive 90/496/EEC, Commission Directive 1999/10/EC, Directive 2000/13/EC of the European Parliament and of the Council, Commission Directives 2002/67/EC and 2008/5/EC and Commission Regulation (EC) No 608/2004 Text with EEA relevance
Select: 1

OJ L 304, 22.11.2011, p. 18–63 (BG, ES, CS, DA, DE, ET, EL, EN, FR, IT, LV, LT, HU, MT, NL, PL, PT, RO, SK, SL, FI, SV) This document has been published in a special edition(s) (HR)
• In force
Current consolidated version: 01/01/2018
CELEX number: 32011R1169
Form: Regulation

You will be taken to the HTML and PDF formats currently in force, which you may access in the language of your choice, in our case it will be English (EN).

http://tiny.cc/owsrxz

On the left-hand side of the page, prior to clicking on the HTML or PDF format, you will see the history of all versions of this Regulation, from when it was first published to the current version. This info comes under "Show all versions".

If you wish to share the document, you have the option to do so in the right corner of the page.

If you need to access a Directive instead, simply replace letter R with letter L in your search box.

How to construct a Product Brief

This can be done in many shapes and forms, and I have provided an example below:

Please provide the **name of the product**-this is the name of the item that you want NPD team to develop.

Strawberry yoghurt

What is the **benchmark**-this refers to any similar product currently available on the market that can be referenced.

The name of the product being referenced

Does the product need to contain **natural flavours**-this pertains to the status of this type of ingredients, as in natural or non-natural.

Yes

Is **fruit depiction** needed on the label-it relates to the imagine of a fruit / botanical /spice / flower displayed on the label.

Yes – strawberry

Is ingredient **provenance** required-it refers to a specific region from which an ingredient originates, e.g., Valencian orange.

No

Are any **claims** mentioned on the label-the term concerns any type of label statement intended to persuade the consumer to purchase the product.

Plant-based
With live cultures
Source of calcium
Rich in plant protein
Dairy & gluten free

Does the product need to cover any **dietary requirements**–it applies to consumers with a specific type of diet, e.g., vegetarian, ovo-lacto vegetarian, vegan, kosher, halal, celiac, lactose intolerant.

Yes–suitable for vegan, celiac and lactose intolerant diets

Is the product **allergen** free – this makes reference to the fourteen allergens (for EU & UK) that can be present in food / drinks.

No–contains soya

When is the product needed for **approval**–this refers to the date of having the product already developed and ready for the first assessment by the customer.

Date

What is the production **launch date** for the product–it alludes to the approximate date on which the product will be made on the production line.

Date

Name of the person who requested the development work.

Name

Date of request.

Date

New Product Development Checklist

Whenever you develop a new product, it is imperative that you conduct thorough checks to ensure that it meets the brief, and that it conforms to the regulations of the market in which it is being developed.

In this regard, I have provided an example of an alcoholic beverage and the checks that can be conducted. As most of these aspects have already been addressed in the book, I will not elaborate further on them.

Name of the product: Cherry Rum & Diet Cola Drink 5% abv

Development draft recipe reference number: 1150

To be checked	EU regulations and the brief's requirements	New developed product
Allergen status	Allergen free	yes
Natural claims	All flavours used must be natural	yes
Depiction on the label	Cherry flavour	yes
Provenance on any of the ingredients	No	n/a
Dietary requirements	Suitable for Vegetarians / Vegans; Energy reduced	yes
Market suitability	Suitable for the EU market	yes
Propylene Glycol level	< 1000 mg/L	780 mg/L
Triacetin / diacetin / triethyl citrate level	< 3000 mg/kg (individually or in combination *)	0 mg/kg
Dyes level		n/a (caramel colouring is used instead)
Quinine level		n/a
Caffeine level	< 150 mg/L	5 mg/L

Sweetener level	Steviol glycosides expressed as steviol equivalents < 150 mg/L	27 mg/L
Glycyrrhizinic acid level		n/a
Polyol level		n/a
Phenylalanine level		n/a
Other		n/a

* *Please refer to "PART 4 – Food additives including carriers in food flavourings" screenshot, within "How to calculate how much propylene glycol (PG) is coming from the flavours" chapter to understand what the 3000mg/kg limitation applies to.*

Checked by: _____

Date: _____

How to build a Procedure

For a more professional appearance, you may want to include the following information in the header of the page: **Logo of the company, Name of the procedure, Document no., Date, Issue no., Issued by, Approved by.**

The following procedure outlines the Approval Process for a New Ingredient.

Procedure's objective:

- Assuring that the correct steps are followed so that a new ingredient can be approved.
- The ingredient is suitable for the intended purpose.

Reference documents:

- Ingredient Technical Data Sheet
- Ingredient Allergen Declaration
- Ingredient Safety Data Sheet

Tasks to be completed:

- Obtain Technical Data Sheet, Allergen Declaration and Safety Data Sheet from the supplier and have these checked.
- Assess the new ingredient from an organoleptic perspective, by making samples with it. You may need to compare this ingredient to another ingredient of the same type you have already purchased from another source.
- Having determined that the proposed ingredient meets the approval criteria, communicate this back to the supplier.
- Set this up on your company's system and let the business know.

Aspects to be considered:

- When checking the Allergen Declaration make sure you are not introducing a new allergen onto the site, and that you are following your company's internal procedure on allergens.

- In assessing the Technical Data Sheet, ensure that the product corresponds with the capabilities and methods of manufacture of your business.

How to put together a Process Diagram for the department

The following information may be useful to include in the header of your document for a more polished image: Logo of the company, Name of the process diagram, Document no., Date, Issue no., Issued by, Approved by.

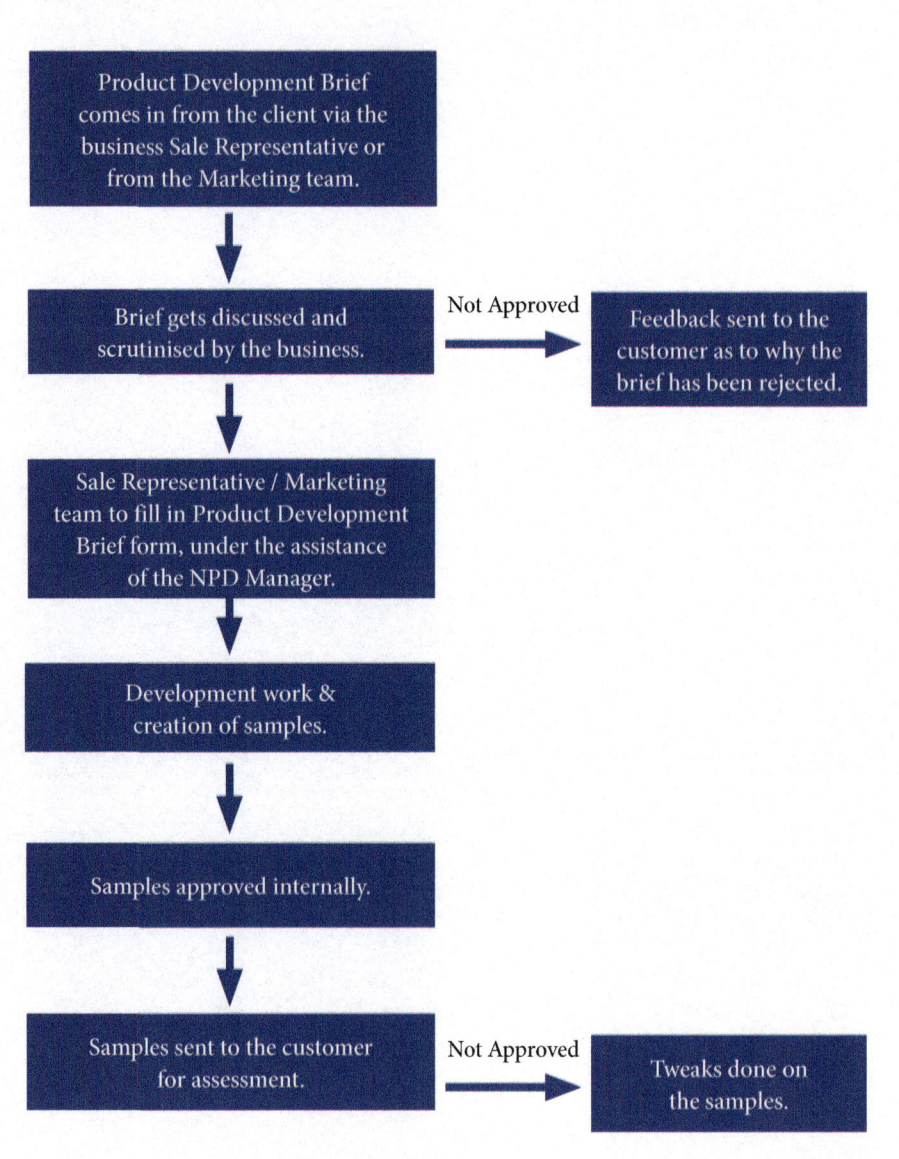

```
┌─────────────────────────────┐
│ Product Development Brief   │
│ comes in from the client via│
│ the business Sale           │
│ Representative or from the  │
│ Marketing team.             │
└──────────────┬──────────────┘
               ▼
┌─────────────────────────────┐   Not Approved   ┌─────────────────────────────┐
│ Brief gets discussed and    │ ───────────────▶ │ Feedback sent to the        │
│ scrutinised by the business.│                  │ customer as to why the      │
└──────────────┬──────────────┘                  │ brief has been rejected.    │
               ▼                                 └─────────────────────────────┘
┌─────────────────────────────┐
│ Sale Representative /       │
│ Marketing team to fill in   │
│ Product Development Brief   │
│ form, under the assistance  │
│ of the NPD Manager.         │
└──────────────┬──────────────┘
               ▼
┌─────────────────────────────┐
│ Development work &          │
│ creation of samples.        │
└──────────────┬──────────────┘
               ▼
┌─────────────────────────────┐
│ Samples approved internally.│
└──────────────┬──────────────┘
               ▼
┌─────────────────────────────┐   Not Approved   ┌─────────────────────────────┐
│ Samples sent to the customer│ ───────────────▶ │ Tweaks done on              │
│ for assessment.             │                  │ the samples.                │
└─────────────────────────────┘                  └─────────────────────────────┘
```

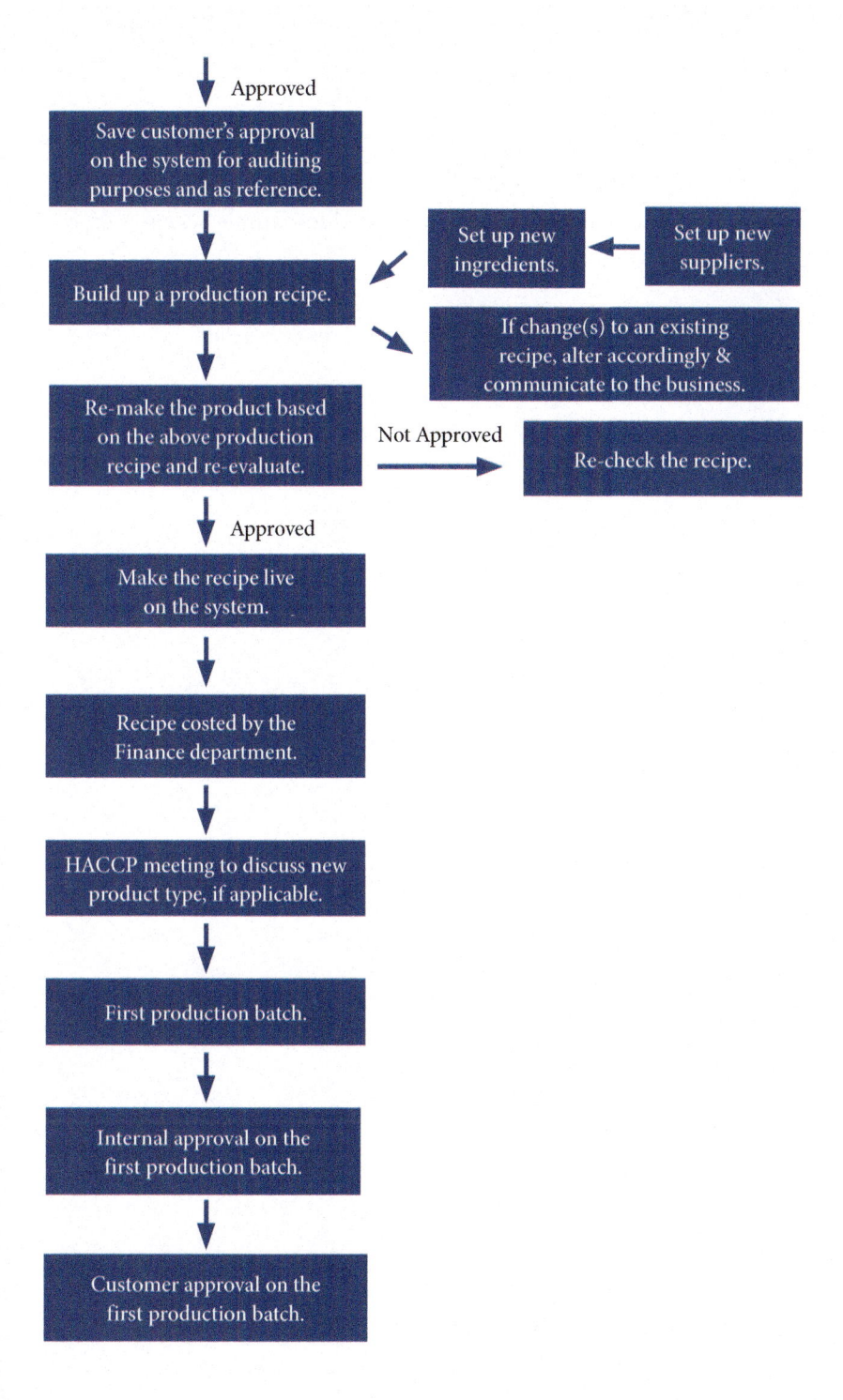

```
                    ↓ Approved
        ┌─────────────────────────┐
        │ Save customer's approval │
        │ on the system for auditing│
        │ purposes and as reference.│
        └─────────────────────────┘
                    ↓                          ┌──────────────┐      ┌──────────────┐
                                               │ Set up new   │ ←──  │ Set up new   │
                                               │ ingredients. │      │ suppliers.   │
        ┌─────────────────────────┐    ↙       └──────────────┘      └──────────────┘
        │ Build up a production    │
        │ recipe.                  │            ┌─────────────────────────────┐
        └─────────────────────────┘    ↘       │ If change(s) to an existing  │
                    ↓                          │ recipe, alter accordingly &  │
                                               │ communicate to the business. │
        ┌─────────────────────────┐            └─────────────────────────────┘
        │ Re-make the product based│   Not Approved
        │ on the above production  │   ──────────────→   ┌─────────────────────┐
        │ recipe and re-evaluate.  │                     │ Re-check the recipe.│
        └─────────────────────────┘                     └─────────────────────┘
                    ↓ Approved
        ┌─────────────────────────┐
        │ Make the recipe live     │
        │ on the system.           │
        └─────────────────────────┘
                    ↓
        ┌─────────────────────────┐
        │ Recipe costed by the     │
        │ Finance department.      │
        └─────────────────────────┘
                    ↓
        ┌─────────────────────────┐
        │ HACCP meeting to discuss new│
        │ product type, if applicable.│
        └─────────────────────────┘
                    ↓
        ┌─────────────────────────┐
        │ First production batch.  │
        └─────────────────────────┘
                    ↓
        ┌─────────────────────────┐
        │ Internal approval on the │
        │ first production batch.  │
        └─────────────────────────┘
                    ↓
        ┌─────────────────────────┐
        │ Customer approval on the │
        │ first production batch.  │
        └─────────────────────────┘
```

Note:

- If a totally new product, a laboratory sample will be used as reference when assessing the first production batch.
- For the next batches, a production product sample is kept after each run and used as a reference.

How to create a Training Record for the department

Procedure's Number	Procedure's Name	Employee's Name			
		A	B	C	D
NPD-1	Glassware Control Procedure	✓	✓	✓	✓
NPD-2	Handling Spillage Procedure	✓	✓	✓	✓
NPD-3	Handling Caustic Soda Procedure	✓	✓	✓	✓
NPD-4	How to use the Balance Procedure	✓	✓	✓	✓
NPD-5	How to use the Mixer Procedure	✓	✓	✓	✓
NPD-6	How to use the Homogeniser Procedure	✓	✓	✓	⌛
NPD-7	Generate Samples Procedure	✓	✓	✓	✓
NPD-8	How to use the Pilot Plant Procedure	✓	✓	✓	⌛
NPD-9	New Supplier Approval Procedure	✓	✓	✓	⌛
NPD-10	New Ingredient Approval Procedure	✓	✓	✓	⌛
NPD-11	Product Shelf-Life Procedure	✓	✓	✓	✓
Food safety	Food Safety & Hygiene in Manufacturing	✓	✓	✓	✓
Allergen Awareness	Food Allergen Training	✓	✓	✓	✓
COSHH	COSHH Training	✓	✓	⌛	⌛

Cost saving ideas

Here are a few cost saving ideas to consider, and depending on your industry, you may be able to employ some of them:

- find an alternative supplier for the item in question (with same / very similar characteristics) who can offer a better price.

- consider using existing ingredients or flavours in your development work rather than introducing new ones.

- some ingredients can be omitted completely from the recipe without affecting the final product. A situation like this rarely occurs, since there is usually a reason for adding an ingredient, however, it is always a good idea to verify.

- study existing recipes and see if you can make improvements by decreasing the amount of processing that is currently needed.

- analyse the forecast for the ingredients for the whole year and determine whether purchasing them in a larger quantity might result in a lower price. You will need to consider the ingredients' shelf life when doing this exercise.

Here are more ideas:

- in some cases, you may be able to substitute some acids that are more expensive for cheaper ones. For example, citric acid is normally cheaper than tartaric acid.

- look at having some of the flavours matched. You might consider having flavours that are widely demanded in Production matched by another flavour house at a cheaper price.

- sometimes, you will purchase ingredients from an agent or middleman, but if you are able to purchase them directly from the manufacturer, you may be able to save money.

- it may be possible again, if you have an ingredient that has a high MOQ (minimum order quantity), to find a match with a lower MOQ and thus save on waste.

- try reducing some of the ingredients' dosage by a small amount or percentage and see if colleagues are able to detect the difference. You might consider conducting a tringle test to determine how easy or difficult it is to detect this change.

How to help the environment ideas

Here are a few ideas that may be useful to you, depending on the industry you are in and the technologies available:

- recycle or re-use packaging materials whenever possible (cardboard, IBCs, plastic bottles etc).

- examine whether it is possible to extend the shelf life of an expired ingredient by a few more weeks or months (if applicable).

- assess existing processing techniques to determine if they can be improved by utilizing less water or energy.

- consider printing on both sides of the paper if applicable, or consider going paperless. If so, obtain electronic signatures for your documents.

- if you're making a brew at work, only use what you need and avoid wasting water and energy.

- look at the possibility of planting trees, shrubs, or flowers on site.

Here are more ideas:

- collect rainwater for use in flushing toilets.

- use solar panels to capture sun's energy.

- install a wind turbine on site for the generation of green electricity.

NPD functionality assessment

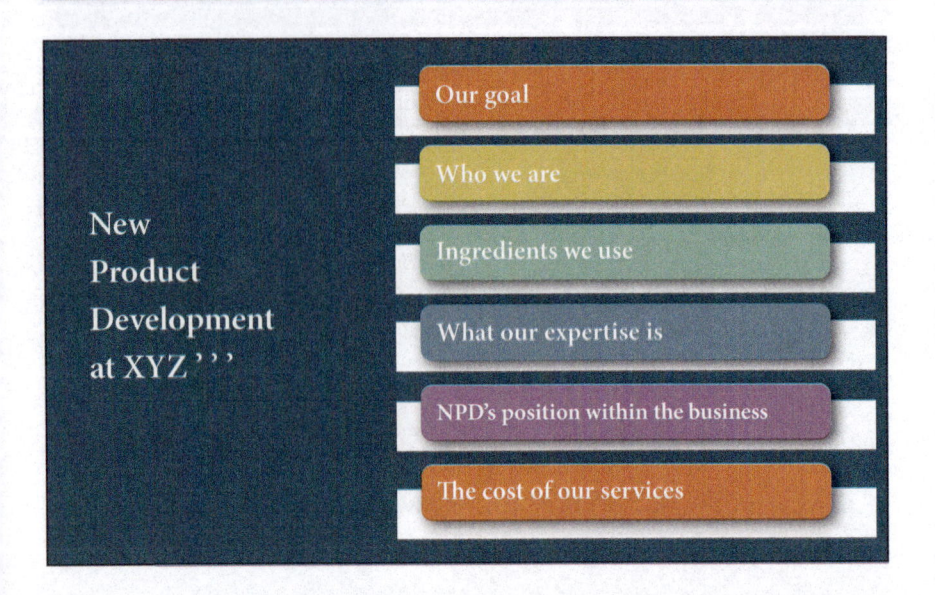

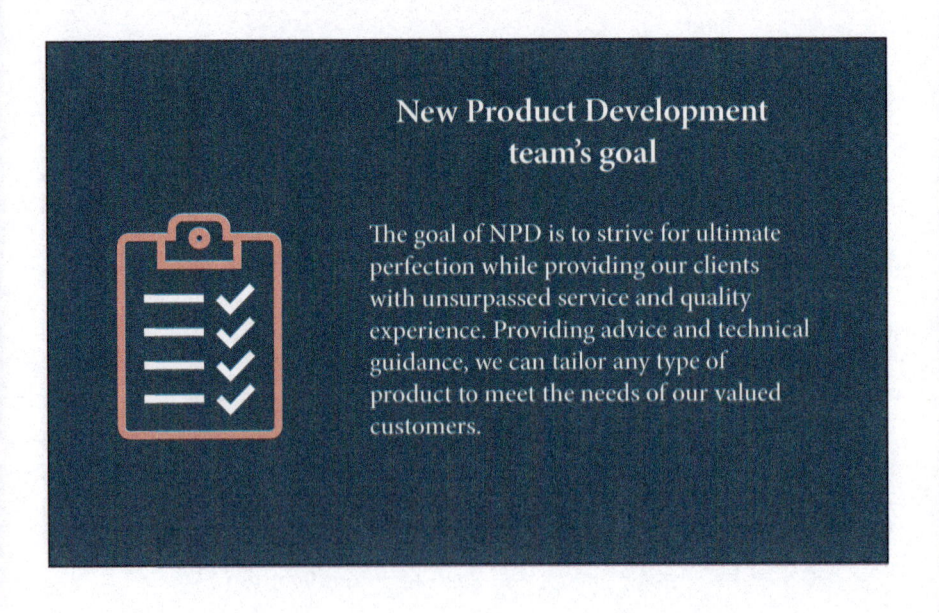

New Product Development at XYZ ''''

- Our goal
- Who we are
- Ingredients we use
- What our expertise is
- NPD's position within the business
- The cost of our services

New Product Development team's goal

The goal of NPD is to strive for ultimate perfection while providing our clients with unsurpassed service and quality experience. Providing advice and technical guidance, we can tailor any type of product to meet the needs of our valued customers.

Who we are

With an emphasis on sustainability, we describe ourselves as being highly motivated and very focused, extremely creative and possessing the ability to think outside the box when needed, offering a unique perspective on the project. Additionally, our commitment to providing excellent customer service goes beyond our passion for innovation.

The NPD team has a combined experience of more than 70 years in the field, demonstrating its commitment to quality and success through the use of science as the main engine of growth.

Ingredients we use

Throughout our development process, the NPD team has built deep-rooted relationships with suppliers from around the world, based on confidentiality and trust, that allow us to source some of the finest high-quality ingredients available.

As a result of utilizing natural flavours, we are able to create products that are delicious as well as authentic, which we believe will lead our customers to achieve great commercial success.

What our expertise is

Within our service we offer professional expertise and legal guidance, which in turn will deliver a safe and compliant product for our customers, in a highly regulated market.

Our expertise lies within the below type of products, which can also be manufactured and packed on the company's site:

- Bread
- Croissants
- Cupcakes
- Pretzels
- Pasta

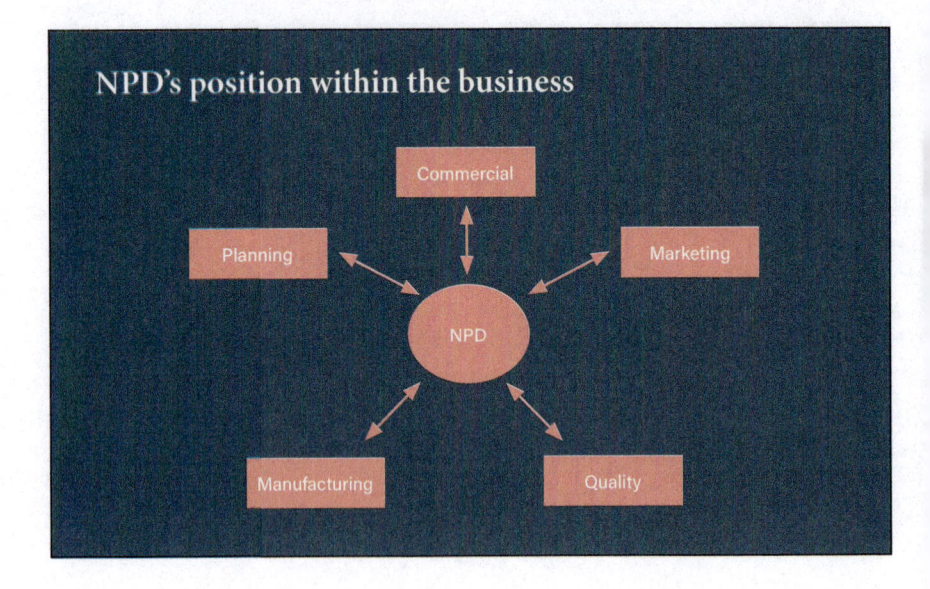

NPD's position within the business

- Commercial
- Planning
- Marketing
- NPD
- Manufacturing
- Quality

The cost of our services

1. Discussion about project feasibility - £

This involves an overview of the technical aspects of the product that needs to be developed, regulatory requirements, the target market, timelines, and the number of samples that need to be submitted.

2. Actual development work and creation of samples - £

This entails developing not more than three similar products using the same base and sending them to the customer for selection.

3. Tweak one & tweak two done on the product, based on customer's feedback - £

This includes maximum two teaks on the product that was developed and submitting these to the customer for final approval. It also involves a recipe set up and compiling a full ingredient list.

Strategy for NPD department

WHERE ARE WE NOW?

WHERE DO WE WANT TO GO?

(This is a strategy model for a flavoured beer manufacturer)

About NPD

As a technical services provider, we are able to create a wide variety of products based on the specifications and preferences of our customers. We describe ourselves as a highly dedicated team, extremely innovative when needed, and bound by an eco-friendly philosophy. Also with a strong scientific background, this gives us an edge when working on complex projects, which often requires a return to chemistry taught back in the day.

In order to source some of the finest high-quality ingredients for our development work, the NPD team has nurtured long-term relationships with selected global suppliers based on a mutual trust and confidentiality. Using natural flavours enables us to create products that are both authentic & delicious, which we believe will undoubtedly bring great commercial success to our customers.

The scope of our services encompasses professional expertise as well as legal guidance, which, in turn, will deliver a safe and compliant product to our customers, within a highly regulated environment.

Our strategy motto is...

"A satisfied customer is the best business strategy of all."

Michael LeBoeuf

What colleagues and customers say about NPD

Just another positive meeting with the customer.
In essence, he was very impressed with the quality of what we sent him and we may be able to secure a listing because of it.
Laura Gaze

Thanks to your assistance, he has now gained a better understanding of the calculation methodology and accepts that the concentration of some preservatives exceeds the EU standards.
Jasmine Norton

It is great to hear that the blending was complete without any issues!
Matt Johnson

I am very impressed with the attention to detail and the technical support NPD provides to ensure that the products are within legal requirements.
Sam Greaves

Well done NPD, you are doing a great job!
Danny White

It has been a pleasure working with you both and I am grateful for the hard work you have put into this project.
Jack Mackenzie

Thank you for your patience with this - much appreciated.
Fiona Rahman

NPD - As ever, the liquid was awesome. According to the buyer, the liquid profile was great and it stood out from the competition.
Mark Doran

Market analysis - Competition

Type of business:
Company A - Beer Manufacturer

About the business:
We operate a highly efficient, FSSC 22000, sustainably-powered brewery that produces and packages beer in both bottles and cans.

Our focus remains innovation, and on board with a strong technical backup we have developed a variety of flavoured beers to satisfy everyone's palate.

In terms of the environment, the purpose of our mission is to preserve water, accelerate the transition to a low carbon world, and design a sustainable future for our planet. Water efficiency has already been improved by 40% in our operations, and every beer we make uses on average 25% less water, compared to previous years. Also, a new wind turbine at our facility has assisted us in transferring 50% of our energy to wind power.

Market analysis - Competition

Type of business:
Company B - Beer Manufacturer

About the business:
As a leading innovator in the field of flavoured beers as well as quality imported beers, we have a wide range of both branded products as well as private label.

We provide a wide range of services to our customers, from a small to a large scale, including:

- Liquid development;
- Bottling services;
- Laboratory and quality assurance.

Integrating sustainable business practices into all aspects of our strategy is at the core of what we do. Across our entire organization, we have achieved carbon neutrality status, 95% of our packaging being fully recyclable.

Market and consumer insights

Reduced / low / sustainable remain important topics across beer category

Vegan	38%
Sustainable	31%
Ease of use	26%
Environmentally friendly	26%
Low / Non-alcoholic beer	25%
Kosher	12%

Our goals and how to achieve these

What do we want to achieve next?	How do we want to achieve this?	What do we need to achieve this?
► Improve profitability and expand the business by working on more projects channelled through existing settings ► Ensure that the highly skilled and knowledgeable staff remain motivated ► Identify innovation opportunities for the environment. Explore the possibility of creating alcohol from bread that is unfit for human consumption in order to reduce food waste ► Use microalgae to capture CO_2 produced by the fermentation process and convert it into oxygen	► Maintain a commitment to providing valuable advice and support, both to the customer and the business ► Go on relevant courses ► Maintain brainstorming meetings with the NPD team to encourage greater employee involvement ► Use our technical expertise (research work, lab ferments, making samples up) to determine what is achievable ► Engage universities that have conducted studies on this topic and collaborate with them	► It is feasible to accomplish this with current team members, but this could change ► Allocate the money for the course ► Facilitate / give time for this to happen ► Time ► Possible more resources ► Obtain the support of retailers for the project and establish a contiguous relationship with them ► Time ► Research work ► Equipment

Creating beer from out of date bread

Advantages

- In addition to reducing food waste, it will have a positive impact on the environment as well
- The Project will bring attention from our customers to realise we are a company of the moment with a passion to move things forward to help the Planet
- Working on this project will motivate colleagues to give them a greater sense of purpose and motivation
- We could lead the way with minimal competition

Implementation Strategy

- As this will be a new initiative for the business, there may be a need for additional resources/time allocated
- There may be logistical obstacles to overcome

Companies that use not fit for consumption bakery products to create alcoholic drinks

- Using **day old bagels** as raw material, a Californian distillery has created **whiskey**.

- From **leftover stale bread**, a Belgian brewery has created a craft **beer**.

- An American **vodka** manufacturer uses **baked goods**, that would otherwise be destined for landfills, to create their craft.

- To make their award-winning **beer**, an English brewery rescues **day old bread** from bakeries and **the heel ends of bread** from sandwich factories.

- A brewery in America makes **beer** from **past-its-prime produce**, to reduce food waste.

Use microalgae to capture CO_2 from the beer making to be converted into oxygen

Advantages
- Algae are known to fix carbon dioxide, which potentially can make the fermentation a more carbon neutral process
- This has been trialled by a few breweries and implemented successfully
- There is technical support available from Universities who have done research work in this field
- Site's effluent water quality could improve by feeding some of the organic matter (nitrogen and phosphorous) to algae
- The old algae can be used as a fertiliser/compost ingredient

Implementation Strategy
- Due to the newness of this endeavour, there may be a need for additional resources or time
- There will be a demand for new equipment
- The success of this project will depend on the collaboration of other departments within the company

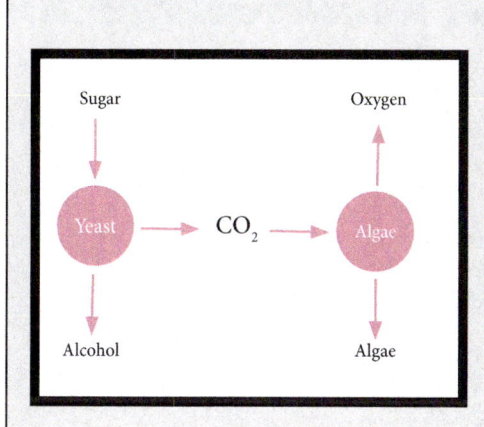

Sugar → Yeast → CO_2 → Algae → Oxygen
Yeast → Alcohol
Algae → Algae

Use microalgae to capture carbon dioxide from the fermentation process, to be converted into oxygen

There is increasing evidence that microalgae can play an important role in rescuing our planet.

During the photosynthesis process algae convert carbon dioxide into oxygen.

Additionally, the algae that it is produced from absorbing all that carbon dioxide can be transformed into food or bioplastics, which can be used in many industries.

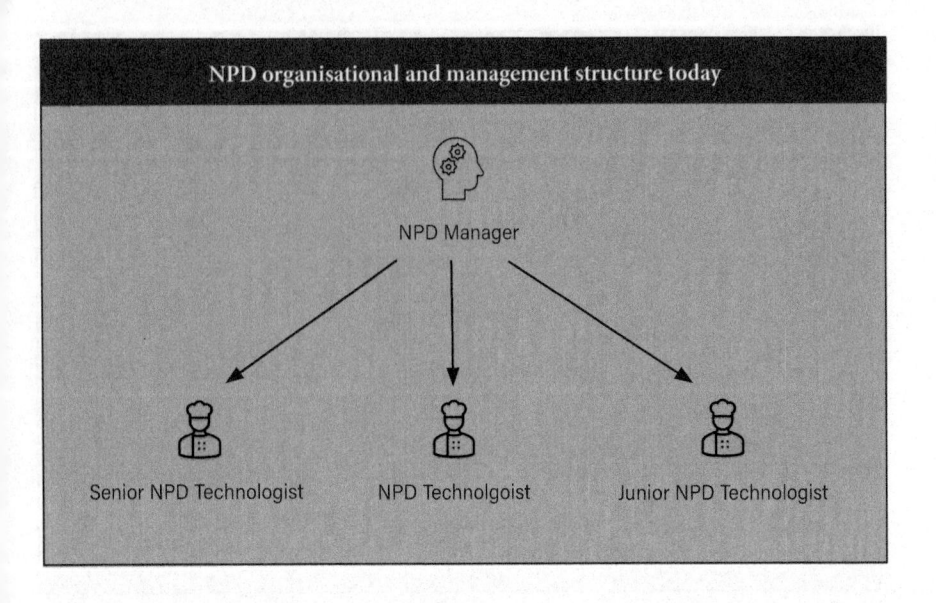

NPD organisational and management structure today

- **NPD Manager**
  - Senior NPD Technologist
  - NPD Technolgoist
  - Junior NPD Technologist

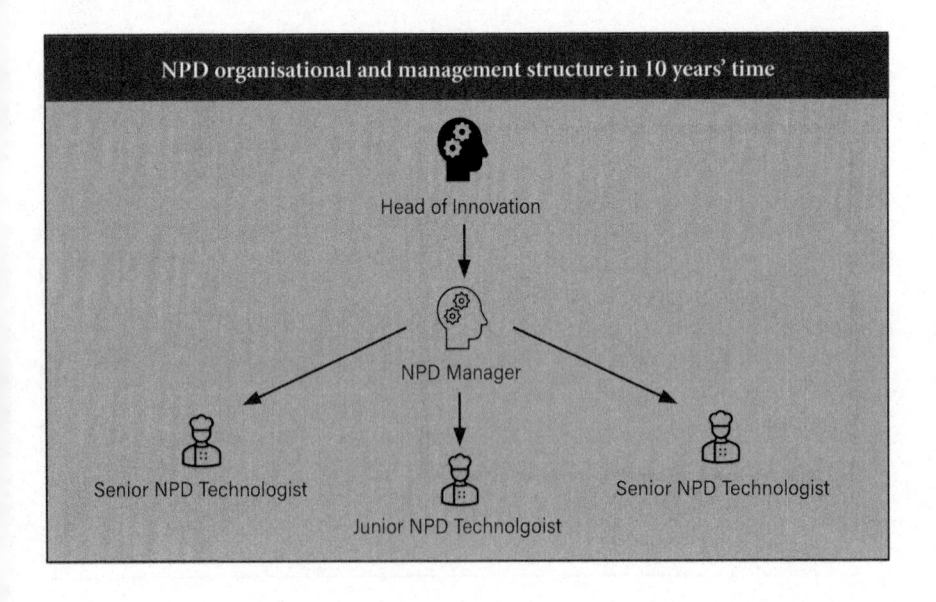

NPD organisational and management structure in 10 years' time

- **Head of Innovation**
  - **NPD Manager**
    - Senior NPD Technologist
    - Junior NPD Technolgoist
    - Senior NPD Technologist

Financial projection

Annual growth rate for beer category on a global scale – volume in million litres

Beer Category	2021	2022	2023	2024F	CR 2021-2022	CAGR 2021-2024F
Dark Beer	8.9	9.3	9.8	11	4.6%	5%
Ale	4.6	4.9	5.1	5.7	4.8%	3.9%
Sorghum	1.4	1.3	1.3	1.4	7.5%	0.6%
Wheat Beer	2.8	3.1	3.4	4.3	10.4%	8.1%
Flavoured Beer	3.4	3.4	3.6	4	1.7%	3.6%
Standard Beer	168	171	174	180	1.9%	1.4%
Stout	1.9	2	2.1	2.4	3.9%	4.8%

Legend:
F = forecast
CR = changing rate
CAGR = compound annual growth rate

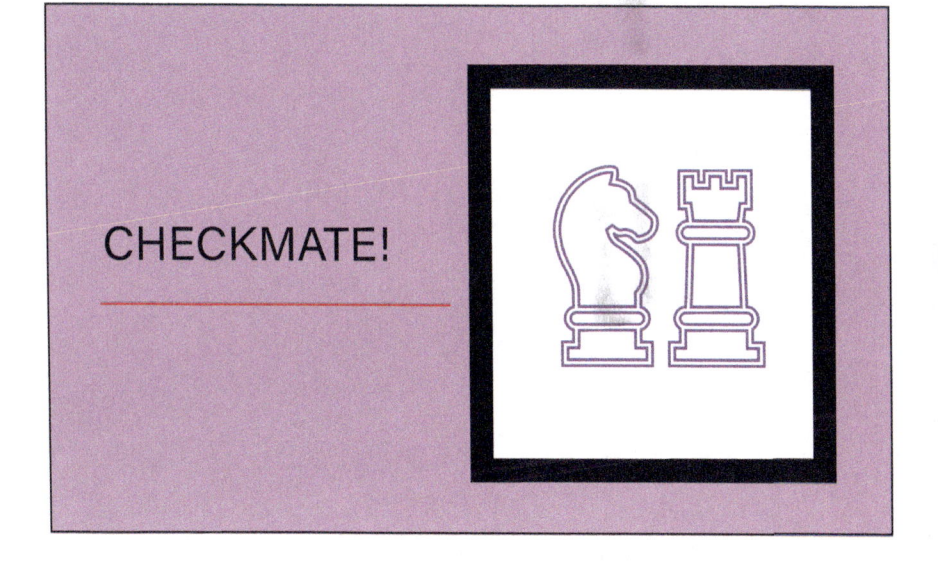

CHECKMATE!

Printed in Great Britain
by Amazon